A
FAITH
❧FOR❧
SKEPTICS

ACW Press
Eugene, Oregon 97405

Scripture quotations are taken from the King James Version of the Bible.

A Faith for Skeptics
Copyright ©2004 John H. Heidt
All rights reserved

Cover Design by Alpha Advertising
Interior design by Pine Hill Graphics

Packaged by ACW Press
85334 Lorane Hwy
Eugene, Oregon 97405
www.acwpress.com
The views expressed or implied in this work do not necessarily reflect those of ACW
Press. Ultimate design, content, and editorial accuracy of this work is the responsibil-
ity of the author(s).

Library of Congress Cataloging-in-Publication Data
(Provided by Cassidy Cataloguing Services, Inc.)

Heidt, John H.

  A faith for skeptics / John H. Heidt. -- 1st ed. -- Eugene, Oregon :
ACW Press, 2004.
    p. ; cm.
    ISBN: 1-932124-21-7

  1. Apologetics. 2. Theology. 3. Skepticism. I. Title.

BT1103 .H45 2003
239-dc22   0311

Printed in the United States of America.

> *I've always been a skeptic. I instinctively disbelieve almost everything, but because I disbelieve much I find it possible to believe.*
>
> Malcolm Muggeridge
> *The End of Christendom*

In Memoriam

Edward C. Lewis
Homer F. Rogers

Contents

Part I

The Heart's Desire

1

The Case of the Disappearing Atheists

Most of us have known people who have an unshakable faith that no doubt can dismay nor reason disturb. Militant defenders of their own private opinions against every critical assault, they eagerly do battle with anyone who dares have ideas or convictions different from their own. In some ways we rather envy their confidence. We hear ourselves saying, "If only I could have a faith like that." Yet their very confidence also bothers us. They seem so imprisoned in their own beliefs. Whether talking about politics, morality, or religion, they are so convinced they are right that no new or uncomfortable fact can penetrate their minds. For them there is nothing new to be learned or more questions to be asked. Behind their certainty lies a benign innocence, yet one that turns deadly in the minds and hands of terrorists or serial murderers.

At the other extreme are those people who appear incapable of believing in anything whatsoever. Far from defending their private opinions, they take pride in their invincible doubts. Always searching after the truth, they seldom ever find it, and would undoubtedly deny it if they did. They too have nothing to learn, for they are as dogmatic about their doubts as others are opinionated in their beliefs. Both live out their lives on a stage of absolute certainties where rational discourse finds little place.

You, however, are more than likely among that vast majority of people who are neither so clear about their faith nor dogmatic about their doubts. Though you would like to believe in something worthwhile, you don't know where to look or what questions to ask.

You search for a certitude that is not opinionated and a faith that can grow by questioning. Perhaps you latch on to the latest philosophical fad or plunge yourself into esoteric forms of meditation. You may have sat at the feet of a self-appointed millennium prophet or listened compulsively to the newest TV evangelist.

Then to your dismay you discover that prophets and evangelists have feet of clay, that philosophical fads quickly become passé, and that meditation by itself fails to solve the pressing problems of everyday life. You continue to search desperately for something to believe in, but you have no idea which way to turn and are tempted to give up the search.

Overcoming a Bad Press

This search for something worthwhile to believe in may seem hopeless, not because you have given up the search too soon but because you have searched too hard and in all the wrong places. The fulfillment of your heart's desire may not be in some esoteric or secret place but in your own household or in the heart of your next-door neighbor or perhaps in the building just around the corner from your own home. It may be that the only thing worth believing is to be found in an ancient but common body of beliefs known as traditional Christianity.

In searching for a faith you can live by, you may have dismissed Christianity simply because you think you already know what self-professed Christians are like and want nothing to do with them. Or you may think that traditional Christian beliefs have all been proven wrong and are not worth considering. For some people the very word "Christian" stirs up images of ancient superstitions, dreary sermons, or Bible-thumping fanatics ready to hit anyone over the head who is having a good time.

Let's face it. Christianity *has* had a bad press. Many people have picked up all sorts of wrong impressions about the Christian faith, either from ill-informed Christians or from a prejudiced mass media. You may be one of them. But why rely on prejudice and misinformation? Why not go to those who are supposed to know what they are talking about? Why not go to the professionals? After all, if you want to know something about medicine, you ask a doctor, and if you want to learn about cooking, you go to a good cook. You go to a physicist to find out about physics and to a musician to study music. Instead of relying on hearsay from self appointed experts, you get the facts straight from the horse's mouth, from professionals who know what they are talking about.

A Professional Christian

That's why I decided to write this book. I am a professional Christian, a Christian priest and parish pastor, and I am supposed to know what I am talking about. Yet I know that this will almost certainly not reassure you. If being a committed Christian puts some people off, being a professional Christian is even more likely to do so. Why, after all, should you pay any attention to someone who is paid for his beliefs?

For one reason. Though it is true that I am paid for my beliefs, I do not believe *because* I am paid. I could make more money selling insurance or flying airplanes. It is certainly not enough money to make me sell my soul or destroy my intellectual integrity. I do not believe in order to have a cushy job or financial security. Financial pressure has not made me a Christian. Nor do I believe out of fear. Neither personal threats, political coercion, nor family pressure has forced me to believe the way I do. If I should renounce my Christian faith, I am not afraid that my wife will sue for divorce, my children leave home, or the police arrest me for high treason.

My Christian faith is very personal to me, but though it is personal it is anything but private. If it was just a private matter, there is no reason why anyone else should bother about it. Those who base their lives on private beliefs are not really faithful but opinionated, and most people are too worried about their own opinions and too caught up in their own beliefs to care that much about the opinions of anyone else.

But my beliefs are not really mine. I did not make them up out of my own head. Though very personal to me, they are shared by a great many others. They are in the public domain and are available to anyone who cares to examine them. They are not my invention but my inheritance, culled from a great variety of public sources. And I accept them because, as with so many who have gone before me, these particular beliefs make more sense to me than anything else and give me a practical guide for my everyday life. I am a believing Christian because the facts of life and common sense compel me to believe the way I do, not because I am paid to believe.

The Joy of Disbelief

This is not to say that I always enjoy being a Christian, or any other kind of religious believer for that matter. In some ways it might be a lot more fun and perhaps even more heroic to be an atheist.

In defiance of an inner fear that supernatural powers are trying to control my destiny, there are times I would like to shake my fist at the heavens and cry out to the gods, "I do not need to bow down before you in abject and pitiable servitude. You can no longer dominate my life, for I now know that you are nothing more than the subconscious creatures of my own distorted imagination. What no priest was able to achieve has now been done by the modern psychiatrist who has at last set us free from all our primordial fears." In some such way I dream that I can throw off the shackles of divine domination and assert my independence of the God of the Bible or the gods of ancient myth or any other kind of supernatural being.

At such moments I ask myself if there is still time to join that great company of militant atheists I used to read about at school, famous people like Nietzsche, Shaw, and Bertrand Russell. Then, instead of the present book, I could write a manual of atheism to guide you towards a high adventure of individual freedom reaching far beyond the confines of an ancient and weary Christianity and the subservient pursuit of a God none of us can ever really know.

Yet when I search for interesting nonbelievers, I search in vain. Even if I happen to find a gang of militant atheists, they as likely as not turn out to be a handful of aging socialists or a smattering of bishops approaching retirement. And I ask myself whatever happened to that high adventure of militant disbelief once trumpeted by their faithless forefathers.

Disappearing Atheists

A nightmare sometimes haunts my early waking hours. Dreaming I have just sat down to breakfast, I find next to my bowl of cornflakes a devastating headline staring up at me from the front page of my daily paper.

CONSERVATIONIST SHOCK: EARTH'S LAST ATHEIST DISAPPEARS

At first I fail to take in the implications of the awesome message, but then, as its full meaning gradually dawns, I shudder to think that all those atheists of my younger days are no more. What a terrible loss at cocktail parties where once you could almost always find a couple of them murmuring godless witticisms in secluded corners of the room while others huddled together to share the penetrating insights of Schopenhauer, H.G. Wells, or Jean Paul Sartre. How we shall miss their radical pleas for justice on panel discussions broadcast by the PBS, or their daring exploits into the theater of the absurd. These atheists of a lost generation were a kindly and amusing breed, and life will never be quite the same without them.

In my dream I wonder by what foul deed these atheists of former days suddenly met their end. Could they have been destroyed by a change in the world's climate of opinion as surely as a different sort of climatic change destroyed the dinosaur? Perhaps they were simply knocked on the head by logical argument, or cast to one side by wartime atrocities and crimes against humanity more devastating by far than their own mild disbelief. Many of their most cherished hopes undoubtedly evaporated in the mushroom cloud ascending over Hiroshima.

I may never know what really happened, but I do know that my nightmare has actually come true. The atheists of former days have all but disappeared, even though their disappearance has not been noted by glaring headlines in the popular press. Gone are those heady days when Huxley thought he had shown God His walking papers by creating his nightmare utopia. No longer do we care that Herbert Spencer believed he had blasted God into oblivion with a scientific theory, or Bertrand Russell with a mathematical formula. By now we are only mildly bemused to learn that George Bernard Shaw thought he had sent God to His eternal reward by discovering sin for the first time.

I well remember hearing people heatedly debate the propriety of burying an atheist like Shaw in the sacred precincts of Westminster Abbey, little realizing at the time that they were really debating where to bury an entire age that had imperceptibly come to an end. No longer were we to see great herds of atheists stalking the earth, arguing for justice and equality and human rights. Gone also were the days when they might be found roaming through the lecture halls and drawing rooms of civilized society, carelessly destroying much of the very civilization through which they roamed and knocking down the foundation stones of the very virtues they proclaimed, leaving in their wake—as their only lasting memorial—poverty, despotism, bombed-out buildings, and the bloodstained victims of bullet-splattered schools.

Departing with neither a bang nor a whimper, the old-fashioned atheists just faded away into the mists of history, leaving behind them a chaotic assortment of ideological and political tyrannies built upon their dreary rationalistic philosophy—a philosophy which in itself is now being overthrown by a new revolution no atheist could have ever foretold, a spiritual quest, a touching of angels, and a new paganism. The former atheism is no more, and those who still think of themselves as atheists have an old-fashioned air about them, a certain quaintness eliciting a feeling of nostalgia.

Friends in the Faith

Atheism was born out of the rationalism of the eighteenth century and is no longer a viable option in our postmodern world with its anti-rationalism and spiritual angst. Yet I miss the atheists of former days, for, in spite of all their destructive behavior, they at least believed in something and were definite about what they believed. You could talk with an old-fashioned atheist and know what you were talking about.

On those rare occasions when I have actually met a real atheist I have discovered that our ability to believe in something has given us much more in common than either of us would have imagined. When we argued with one another, we each knew where the other stood. We both stood on the solid ground of faith. My atheist friend may not have liked the idea, but at heart we were long lost friends in the faith. We just disagreed about the object of our faith. The atheist could not put his faith in the existence of God, but this was only because he so passionately believed in the goodness of man. He placed his whole faith in humanity, whereas I had come to place mine in divinity.

It was the atheist's belief in humanity that kept him from believing in God. Unlike so many people today who think that religion is probably a very good thing but have no idea what it is really all about, the old-fashioned atheist believed he knew exactly what religion was all about, and thought it was a very bad thing. He was convinced it was something so destructive that it had to be stamped out at all costs. It seemed to him that all religion, no matter what, was humanity's most dangerous enemy, being built upon a tissue of lies which—though they might comfort some people for awhile—would, if allowed to go unchecked, eventually stifle all human freedom and progress. And to prove his point all he had to do was point an accusing finger at the stake-burned victims of the Grand Inquisitor, the atrocities of the Crusades, Galileo's bigoted judges, or the humiliation of Hester's "A".

Downfall

This exclusive belief in humanity was the atheist's greatest strength and his most attractive asset, but it also led to his eventual downfall. Those intellectual giants who strode across the Victorian landscape were finally seen to be one-legged giants. Throwing their entire weight on the goodness of man and none on the reality of God, they eventually toppled over from the very absurdity of their stance. In the court of rational argument their defense crumbled to the ground once the prosecution pointed out that most of the evidence suggested that mankind was not all that good. And their descendants began to see that if they no longer believed in God, there was little reason for believing in themselves or in anything else for that matter. When atheists proclaimed that God was dead, it was they who died instead, leaving behind them people like ourselves who have nothing left to do but search for new gods and a new faith.

The atheist of former days met his end because he kept asking if God is real when he should have been asking what he meant by "reality." The questions that haunt us are not so much about the existence of God but about the kind of world we live in, questions about the meaning of life and how we are to handle the reality of death, and how to live with all the evil and suffering that weighs us down so unmercifully. Most people today find it much easier to believe in some kind of God than in their own humanity.

Instead of proclaiming that as long as there is evil in the world we cannot possibly believe in God, it would have been much more to the point for the atheist to have asked what kind of God—given all this evil—you and I can possibly believe in.

2

Anonymous Agnostics

Far off in the distance I occasionally think I see someone who still denies the existence of God in order to prove the goodness of man. Following in the footsteps of such great defenders of the faith as C. S. Lewis or Dorothy L. Sayers, I run after these modern atheists with arm upraised, eager to engage them in battle, only to discover, once I catch up with them, that they are nothing like the atheists I had expected to meet. Instead I usually find rather vague and liberal agnostics who have no real interest in proving or denying anything at all, except perhaps the rather obvious fact that there is frightening starvation abroad and unfair prejudice at home.

Though these liberal agnostics seem to have nothing against Christianity, it never occurs to them that Christianity might actually be true. Whereas you could get into a really good argument with an old-fashioned atheist, it is virtually impossible to argue about anything at all with this new breed of unbeliever. With no real interest in logical debate, they take their stand on little more than their own private feelings supported by the weight of a public opinion formed largely by fellow agnostics.

Quicksand Under Our Feet

The old atheist was able to stand his ground, but this new breed of agnostic stands on constantly shifting ground. Start talking to him about the existence of God, and he, likely as not, will counter your arguments by asking why Christians—if they really believe in a good God—should ever get into trouble with the police. If you reply by saying something about temptation and sin, he shifts ground once again by asking how a good God can allow so much evil in the world. Like Alice in Wonderland chasing the White Rabbit, you try to keep up with him by explaining something about free will, divine love, and the work of the devil, but before you have gone more than a few sentences he interrupts by saying that if only the church was doing its job, we would not need the police in the first place. Just when you think you are getting somewhere, you find yourself right back where you started. In trying to find some common ground with your protagonist he keeps throwing sand in your eyes, only for you to discover that by some mysterious sleight-of-hand, the sand in your eyes has turned into quicksand under your feet.

More often than I care to tell, I have felt myself sinking into this quicksand of irrational debate, and in despair I pray that my protagonist will take a def̲i̲n̲i̲t̲e̲ some sort of solid ground of belief, no mat-
tian it may turn out to be.

Vague Unease

ry men and women are not like these new
e to stand; they want something to believe
new agnostics are not really on the wave-
r from wandering the streets with the likes
hiding in modern rectories of halfhearted,
lled together behind dry-as-dust tomes of
spend much of their time doing little else
r what little belief they have left.

not suffer from this pathological fear of
g, the cynicism of these latter-day agnos-
ll rather skeptical of any kind of definite
may be kept from pursuing your natu-
atmosphere of cynical skepticism sur-
n be one of those many thousands
ink, drugs, and sex are not viable alter-
o a permanent state of disillusionment
oned any hope of finding some real

for something to believe in, some god
r trust, the last god you are likely to

Canon John Heidt
50th Anniversary of Ordination
to the Sacred Priesthood

June 2nd, 2007

St. Vincent's Cathedral
Bedford, Texas

Domine, non sum dignus

look at is the God of traditional Christianity, the God worshiped by professing Christians throughout the world, the God you learned something about from the blue rinse brigade of early Sunday school days. The dogmatic doubts of anonymous agnostics, even if not expressed in so many words, have by now created such a sweeping skepticism of Christian belief in the popular imagination that seekers after a living faith are no longer likely to take traditional Christian beliefs very seriously.

The Will to Believe

Death takes the son of your closest friend and for the first time in your life you make a valiant attempt to pray. Just as two world wars taught a whole generation that there are no atheists in foxholes, so now you sadly discover that there are none at the graveside either. You start to pray to whatever god may be out there, but then you imagine you hear one of these anonymous agnostics quietly mocking you. Quickly you give up your attempt as so much childish nonsense brought on by the emotions of the moment, consoling yourself that at least this rough attempt at prayer made you feel better for awhile, even if it didn't do you or anyone else any real or lasting good.

Then there is Sue. She attends an Alpha Course and begins hanging around with friends who call themselves Christians. She begins going to church with them and discovers that she really enjoys the music and ceremonies and the friendship she finds. Sue learns more about the faith that binds these people together, and eventually is baptized and confirmed. But soon she learns the price she has to pay for her newfound faith. Her schoolmates tease her for believing all that nonsense and her nonbelieving parents tell her that if she was such a good Christian she would help more around the house, run errands for them, and never get into any kind of trouble. The anonymous agnostic begins to loom large before her and she stops going to church for fear of being thought a fool.

Brian, a man in his late twenties, suddenly realizes with a lightning flash of unexpected insight, that there must be something more to life than a high-paying job and a bigger house in the suburbs. He rejects the middle-class values of his friends and parents, lets his hair grow long, and begins to grow a scruffy beard. He tries his hand at the guitar with an amateur rock group and experiments with body piercing. He looks into various esoteric forms of eastern mysticism and begins to dabble in the occult. But the one thing Brian never thinks about is Christianity. Those same unidentified agnostics drove that possibility out of his head almost as soon as he was born. Why, after all, pursue what everyone knows was discredited long ago? Why take seriously the beliefs and practices of a 2,000-year-old religion that so many people say is hopelessly out of date and quite irrelevant to the complex problems of modern life?

The Need for Reassurance

Because I believe that Christianity is far from out of date and highly relevant to the problems of our times, I am going to try to dispel all those nagging doubts put into your head by today's anonymous agnostics. But I am not going to offer you every conceivable reason for believing in Christianity. I only hope that I can help you understand a little more of what Christianity is all about, and to see why so many people find in its teachings the sharpest picture of what we are really like as human beings, and what kind of a world we actually live in and how we can live in it peacefully and happily.

Instead of trying to argue you or anyone else into becoming believing Christians, I merely want to reassure you that it is all right to believe. Reassurance rather than argument is what is needed today, and I believe that this reassurance is more likely to come from a clear description of the Christian faith than from a wealth of arguments in its favor.

A Prehistoric Monster

When you first start to look into traditional Christian beliefs, you may come face to face with ideas so strange and foreign to your present way of thinking that they will seem like creatures from an alien world. In bewilderment and confusion, you may shy away from them and try to cling to your old ways. And when this happens, the anonymous agnostic may—in a perverse sort of way—come to your aid by arguing that these newfangled ideas are nothing more than the fossilized bones of a prehistoric monster, and that what may seem strange and awesome in your first encounter are little more than museum pieces of only slight historical interest, "the graves and sepulchers of God," as Nietzsche, the great cynical skeptic of the nineteenth century, liked to say about Christian churches.

Reassured that you have nothing to be afraid of, your original fear may turn into casual curiosity and, as you continue your search into the real meaning of Christianity, this curiosity may eventually turn into familiarity. Then something completely unexpected may happen. To your utter surprise you may find that these new ideas—far from being the yellowing bones of a dead faith—gradually become, almost imperceptibly, the very backbone of your everyday thinking and behavior. What once seemed like a prehistoric monster may well turn out to be a very contemporary friend, giving you greater confidence as you continue to explore a newfound faith. With ideas, as with people, you may discover that familiarity can breed reassurance rather than contempt.

If what I have written helps build up that reassurance I shall be more than satisfied, bearing in mind that I have done little more than provide a skeleton of belief and a few road signs along the royal road of faith. No book and no amount of talk can provide absolute proof of anything. They certainly cannot prove the object of faith. After reading this book you need to put Christianity to the test if you are ever to come to any definite belief. Personal conviction needs the support of rational argument but, in itself, it only comes from personal experience. As with the proverbial pudding, the proof of any argument lies always in the eating.

3

Dangerous Dogmas

No matter how weighty the arguments may be or how powerful our personal experience, we remain skeptical of any claim to absolute truth because we don't want to appear dogmatic. We see whole races persecuted and good people tortured by fanatics driven by their dogmatic fervor. We see irrational dogmas created to provide intellectual defenses for the opinionated and used to support every perverse prejudice. We accept without thinking that dogmas are dangerous, the chief enemy of progress, freedom, and justice. We take in the fear of dogma with our mother's milk and absorb it into our system from the very air we breathe. Simply by believing in something, we fear that we may run the risk of being dogmatic, and take for granted that having an opinion about anything is bound to make us opinionated.

Dogmas are under attack on all sides. Children are allowed to express their views just so long as they don't take them too seriously. Institutional churches are abandoned for being too dogmatic, and their ancient dogmas are held up to ridicule. Dogmas are blamed for every breach of the peace whether at home or abroad. Countries go to war because they are too dogmatic about their convictions and loyalties, and families become dysfunctional because each member sticks to his own dogmatic guns rather than learning the art of compromise.

Compromise, we are told, is the key to peace, and its handmaid is interpersonal dialogue. For the sake of peace and harmony we are expected to give up our most cherished convictions, or at least keep them to ourselves, so that we can more easily get along with one another.

That, at least, is what the modern world has been telling us. But we are now in a postmodern world that isn't quite so sure. It is a world of men and women looking for something to believe in, a brave new world of people searching for new dogmas. You and I belong to this new world, and we need something to believe in, some principles to follow, some standards to uphold, a dogmatic stance to defend, perhaps even to die for.

We must all be dogmatic about something. Even the liberal agnostic is dogmatic about his hatred of dogmatism. His campaign against every sort of dogma is a chimera, a grotesque parody of human thought. Without dogmas we could neither think nor reason, we could not trust anyone or live together in any kind of community. Far from disrupting the peace, we need dogmas to keep the peace. They are the glue that holds society together.

Dogmas to Live By

When I go to our new Tom Thumb supermarket, I am very rarely tempted to hit the cashier over the head. Though we are complete strangers, I am pleased to say that most of our differences are settled quite amicably. If, for example, I purchase eight dollars worth of groceries and she gives me a dollar back for a ten-dollar bill, I need only to point out the mistake and, with an apologetic smile, she hands over the extra dollar. Someone looking on might easily assume that we were long-standing friends who, over the years, had built up an amazing amount of trust in one another. But of course I know that this friendly way of doing business really has nothing to do with friendship. It depends instead upon a commonly held belief in justice and a mutually shared conviction that two and two make four rather than five. Without even thinking about it, we both assume that I ought to be treated fairly and that eight from ten is not one but two.

What an amazingly clever and easy way to keep the peace! By a simple device of arithmetic, combined with a sense of justice, brawls are avoided in supermarkets and riots in the streets.

I sometimes wonder who could have held such sway over the minds of men that even to this day such complete strangers as the cashier and myself willingly sacrifice our own free thought to such impersonal and abstract standards of arithmetic and justice simply for the sake of keeping the peace. Who convinced us that peace is really worth more than a dollar of change?

Not everyone is convinced of course. Some people quite willingly break the peace for the sake of their own private gain. Dashing into supermarkets, often with guns pointed at cashiers and customers, they take what is not rightfully theirs. And others, subtler or less adventurous, try to make eight and one equal ten by fiddling the books. Yet even they are always peering over their shoulder lest they are caught, for they know that though we may at times admire their audacity, we never congratulate them for their honesty. Because they have stolen other people's goods, we universally agree that it is quite right for them to be hauled up before a judge and given their just reward.

The Hero That Never Was

In my imagination I sometimes picture a single capital of the world where, in the central square, a great statue has been erected in honor of that unsung hero who first laid the cornerstone of this civilized behavior by inventing the principles of arithmetic and justice. Or perhaps a brass plaque has been placed in his honor near the tomb of the Unknown Soldier who gave his life to ensure that this civilized behavior might continue to live.

Yet on reflection, I know that my imaginary statue will never be built nor any new plaque placed near the soldier's tomb. For there never was any such person. No one invented the basic principles of arithmetic simply to keep peace in supermarkets. Nor do we punish a man who invents his own arithmetic just because he endangers the peace or rebels against some arbitrary social custom. We punish him because we believe that in some sort of mysterious way his behavior goes against the very nature of things. Whether we like it or not, we accept the principles of arithmetic as facts that every sane person must obey and all ignore at their peril. And what is true of arithmetic is also true of justice and fairness and other good things like honesty and honor and mutual respect for one another. We believe that all these things should be encouraged simply because they are good in themselves, and that injustice and dishonor should be condemned.

Even the criminal who holds up the supermarket submits to the basic dogmas of arithmetic, rarely if ever defending himself by arguing that two and two really do make five. Instead, he argues, in a perverse sort of way, that he had a right to what he stole; that it was a simple matter of justice and the honorable thing to do. It would seem that indeed there is some strange kind of honor even among thieves.

Two Cheers for Doubting Thomas

Let us suppose, however, that someone insists that all this belief in honor and justice and arithmetic is mere superstition—a carryover from more primitive times when the human spirit was confined by the shackles of ignorance and prejudice. If he is right, why not rise up in protest and allow everyone that wild and exotic freedom to proclaim, if they so wish, that two and two really do make five? And while we are at it, why not give everyone the right to believe in dishonor and injustice as well? Instead of condemning those who rebel against society's common beliefs, perhaps the defenders of these beliefs ought to be hauled into court to produce evidence that the principles of arithmetic really are true and that justice really is good and not just a bizarre leftover from the primitive mind.

Surely, a thorough-going agnostic ought to argue that we have progressed to the point where we can be skeptical about all our social attitudes and question every common belief. We are no longer afraid of black cats or black neighbors, nor look for Halloween witches and hippie goblins round every corner; so why not drive out once and for all every other kind of perfidious belief that straightjackets the human spirit? Just as we were once mistaken about the mischievous antics of cats and witches we thought we could see, are we not now much more likely to be mistaken about the goodness of justice and honor and mathematics which no one can see? Having rid the world of one kind of superstition, let us rid the world of these others as well. Let our patron saint be Doubting Thomas who summed up our skepticism once and for all when he proclaimed, "Unless I feel the print of the nails in his hands and feet and put my hand in the hole in his side, I will not believe" (John 20:25).

Sound the battle cry! Down with all unproven assumptions and death to every common belief for which we can find no evidence! Let us call all men of goodwill to join us in this battle against justice and arithmetic and every other kind of dogmatic belief that tramples underfoot our personal freedom.

And yet, no matter how loud the trumpet sounds, few people seem willing to take up the call. For when it comes to the most important things in life, even the modern skeptic turns out to be as dogmatic as everyone else.

And no wonder. We must all be dogmatic about something, even if it is only about our own skepticism. Dogmas, after all, are really nothing more than the basic principles we take for granted as so obviously true that we rarely if ever need to think about them. Rather, they provide the means for thinking about everything else and lay the foundation stones of our common life. Without some sort of dogmas, civilization as we know it would come to an end. Seriously question the basic assumptions of mathematics and the natural sciences will collapse. Undermine our common belief in economic justice and half the world will starve. Deny belief in the basic goodness of our fellow human beings and we will end up in a morass of child abuse, family violence, and international terrorism. Seriously doubt our own innate goodness and we will end up killing ourselves.

Keeping the Peace

It would seem that we can only build up some kind of integrated mental and emotional life on a foundation of facts and values which we do not have to prove because we believe that their truth is self-evident. Without these self-evident truths, or dogmas, there could be no sensible conversation, no advance in our thinking, and no peace with our fellowmen. Dogmas give us a place to stand and a court of appeal by which we can settle our differences. They bind us together in a universe of discourse and community of action without which there would only be chaos and disintegration, both in society and in the individual.

Most of us can take it on the chin if people criticize our work or our ideas; we don't take it for granted that our ideas are always right or our work exquisitely good. But if others attack our right to work or to think, we will stand up for our rights. We believe in the goodness of work and of thinking, just as we take for granted the rightness of freedom and law and democracy.

These are all part of the dogmatic furniture of our lives. They must be defended at all costs; even, perhaps, if they cost us our very lives. We know intuitively that our basic beliefs or dogmas cannot be defended by rational argument alone, and yet they are so important that in defending them many people will resort to violence if necessary. There is no argument against the nudist or the person who chooses not to work, nor can I argue someone out of his prejudices if he refuses to think, nor encourage him to die for his country if he has no sense of patriotism. As with the cashier in the supermarket, all I can do if I am going to get my way is to hit him over the head, and in similar fashion a society can only maintain its way of life by getting rid of all those who threaten its common beliefs.

To secure the peace, every society must burn its heretics either literally or symbolically. People are imprisoned or hounded by the press. In Africa, South America, and Asia dissidents are murdered or they disappear. In the Middle Ages, when our dogmas were mostly theological, the State, with the connivance of the church, burned its religious heretics at the stake. And now that we have given up that practice, we wonder how a church could succumb to such an evil. This is only because our own dogmas are no longer theological but economic and political. We are now free to choose our religious allegiances, no matter how bizarre, but we are not free to choose our style of government in a world where capitalist democracy has become the final court of appeal for settling all our differences. King Demos has replaced the God of the ancient Jews as the foundation of our common life, and we must burn all those who threaten his supreme reign. Though we would no longer dream of burning theological heretics at the stake, Americans in the 1950s felt no compunction in burning the Rosenburghs in the electric chair for revealing the secrets of a capitalist democracy to the communists.

New Dogmas for Old

One particular dogmatic ideology, more powerful by far than our economic and political dogmas, holds such sway over our lives that no one ever dreams of betraying its secrets or undermining its absolute authority. Just as theology was once the science which supported the teaching and practice of church and state, so now we assume that science itself and the scientific method are able to explain everything from religion to social behavior and individual psychology. To question the pronouncements of science is to attack the very foundation of modern life.

Some years ago, when my young son and I were crossing the English Channel, I started to point out to him, as we looked out towards the horizon, that the earth was obviously flat, whereas he kept insisting—in spite of all the evidence to the contrary—that the earth had to be round. It seemed at the time an innocent enough conversation until suddenly a lady in a forward deck chair, who apparently could stand it no longer, turned upon me with looks to kill. I am quite sure she would have turned her looks into action there and then if she had had the means and the courage. I was clearly a dangerous public enemy who, like Socrates of old, was guilty of perverting the youth and disturbing the peace by undermining the very basis of our common life.

She was a dogmatist without knowing it. In appreciating all the marvelous benefits the scientific method has given us, she failed to realize that we get ourselves into trouble when we become dogmatic about everything going by the name of science or assume all our scientific reasoning is reasonable. Like every other human activity, scientific knowledge rests upon certain basic assumptions which cannot themselves be proven by reason. They must be accepted dogmatically and then tested by experience to see if they make sense and if they help us make sense of everything else. But if these, or any of our other dogmatic assumptions are never tested, we can all too easily become dogmatic about the wrong things. Our dogmatism will then prove very dangerous indeed, and all the fears of the anonymous agnostic will be justified.

4

A Misplaced Skepticism

No matter how big a skeptic we may happen to be, we still need a place to stand. We need to be definite about something in order to question everything else. We need to build our lives on certain self-evident truths or dogmatic assumptions that we don't have to think about. Our emotional and mental stability depend upon it.

But when we discover that the self-evident truths we learned from childhood are not so self evident after all, a terrible and even violent struggle wells up within us. We start questioning everything that once seemed so obviously true, until we become afraid to take a stand on anything at all or believe in anything with real conviction. When we learn from bitter experience that not everyone can be president, that friends cannot always be trusted, or that things we once took for granted are not all that certain or secure, the rug is pulled out from under our feet and our world comes crashing down about our heads. Unless we can find new and more appropriate dogmas, our skepticism gives way to cynicism and all meaning and purpose in life is in danger of being swept away.

This traumatic doubting of dogmas sometimes happens with the death of our parents. In spite of all the evidence, most of us live as though our mothers and fathers are going to be around forever. We have been taught from our childhood that thinking otherwise would be morbid. Then the day comes when we have to face the fact that parents really do die along with everyone else and, as our childhood certainties are laid to rest in our parents' grave, the almost unbearable pain of confusion and disillusionment is added to the grief of our personal loss.

The Destruction of Dogmas

So many things we once took for granted now seem incapable of standing up to the test of actual experience. From the time we first discovered that there is no Santa Claus, one false dogma after another has come crashing to the ground until gradually self-confidence has given way to disillusionment and we seem forced to accept the bitter truth that there is no truth. Feeling terribly betrayed we become members of a new generation that holds up former generations to ridicule for having lied not only about Santa Claus and the everlasting presence of our parents but about everything else as well. To save our sanity, we learn to doubt everything we have ever been told and to renounce every dogmatic belief we have ever held.

What is true of us is also true of society as a whole. All those dogmatic beliefs that once provided the cornerstone of our culture are now open to doubt and subject to question. We can no longer assume that our neighbors or our children have been taught the importance of such simple virtues as loyalty, courtesy, or respect. We no longer look for guidance from the ancient wisdom of Aesop's fables, the poetry of Virgil, or even stories from the Bible. Our cultural myths have become little more than pleasant fictions from a more gullible past. Though they may still have some moral value, we assume that they have nothing to do with life as it really is. Having lost the dogmatic foundation of our corporate life, our social stability can no longer be taken for granted. Peace is overcome by violence and every form of community life is threatened by individual self interest.

The New Dogmatism

With all our traditional dogmas under threat, we have become skeptical about almost everything earlier generations once held dear. Yet this has not made us less dogmatic. As paradoxical as it may seem, the new skepticism has made us more dogmatic than ever. We have ended up not only being dogmatic about our skepticism but about most everything else as well. Thinking we take nothing for granted, we take most everything for granted, letting ourselves fall victim to whatever propaganda a financially driven mass media and a manipulated public opinion throw our way.

Our convictions no longer rest on the truth of what is said but on our impression of who says what. Even though doctors constantly come up with new ideas about what is good for us, we place ourselves in their hands as though their latest opinions were infallible. New health diets come on the market almost every day, and yet we eagerly latch onto the latest one as though it was the final solution to a life of self-indulgence. When scientists develop new theories we call it progress, rarely doubting that their latest theory is the correct one. Far from being genuinely skeptical, we have simply substituted fads for principles, media hype for rational argument, and the proclamations of self-styled experts for scientific evidence.

Pagan Skepticism

The ancient pagans were far more skeptical than we are. Because we assume that the sun has to rise every morning whether it likes it or not, we take each morning for granted, but every morning the pagans thanked their gods for making the sun rise once again because they did not think it really had to happen.

We talk about human rights and even animal rights as though their truth is too self-evident to be debated. We think it obvious that democracy is the only just form of government and assume that the United States is its greatest embodiment. So we are amazed to discover that an ancient Greek philosopher actually entertained his guests at dinner parties by making them puzzle out the reasons for believing in such things. Being superstitious dogmatists rather than philosophical skeptics, we have sent serious questions like these out of the social atmosphere of the dining room into the tedium of the classroom, finding the magical puzzles of David Copperfield much more entertaining than the philosophical puzzles of Plato.

What was true of ancient philosophy was also true of science. The ancient Greek was quite capable of inventing the steam engine, but though he enjoyed playing with it as a toy, it never occurred to him to put hundreds of people in carriages behind the engine and carry them across the country. He was fascinated with the way the steam engine demonstrated his belief in certain principles of physics, but he never imagined that the same principles that worked today would necessarily work tomorrow. Even as he performed his experiments, the world was changing. All was in flux and you could count on nothing.

Skeptical Children

You can find this same thoroughgoing skepticism in your own children. They are forever bothering us with their interminable questions because, like Plato of old, they take nothing for granted. "Why does water run downhill and why are trees green?" "Why do birds fly south in winter and why does the sun shine only in the daytime?" Not only do they keep asking questions we don't know how to answer, they ask them at the most impossible moments, when we are in the middle of preparing dinner, talking to friends, or reading the latest novel by John Grisham. So we try to fob them off with the same old reply, "Well, honey, they just do."

Or perhaps you are one of those conscientious parents who take time out to tell your children about the law of gravity or the chemistry of chlorophyll. You may even let them in on the secrets of animal instinct or, if you think they are old enough, explain the rudiments of the solar system. Then to your surprise you discover that once you start explaining these things to your children, they act as though they couldn't care less. It all seems terribly perverse, but the reason is really quite simple. When children ask why trees are green, they are not asking what it is that makes them green but that it is all right for them to be green. Our children are not near as interested in how migrating birds behave, as they are in finding out if it is right for them to behave the way they do. They are not interested in physics but in an ancient science far beyond physics, in something called metaphysics. They are not scientists but philosophers at heart.

Children take nothing for granted because they want to find out the truth about everything. But we find it almost impossible to understand what they are on about because we are blinded by our own unconscious dogmatism. Our dogmas dictate what kind of questions we assume our children ought to ask and what explanations they should accept. But they quickly lose interest in our most carefully thought-out explanations, because our dogmas are not theirs and our thoughts are not their thoughts.

We answer questions that are of no interest to them and offer explanations that explain nothing. What, after all, does instinct tell us about birds except that we have no idea why they fly south in winter, and what is gravity except a shorthand way of saying that everyone, like the child, has noticed that water runs downhill? Instinct and gravity and a host of similar things are modern myths we use to explain the unexplainable. They are mysterious gods we drag in for fear of falling into the abyss of the unknown; dogmas we cling to in the blind hope of filling the gaps in our understanding of a mysterious universe.

A Children's Crusade

Children defend their own integrity by protecting themselves from the onslaught of their parents' dogmas. When little Mary comes home and says she has just seen a lion in the next road, she is expressing the fear and awe she feels when she leaves the security of her immediate neighborhood. But if her father dogmatically insists that there are no lions in the next road, the lion Mary saw will suddenly spring to life with a real mane and a frightening roar, and she will defend its existence even to the point of going to bed without her supper. She knows that her experience of the lion is real and that, for the sake of her own integrity, she dare not kill it off no matter how much pressure is put upon her by her parents. She has the wonder of St. Peter when he wrote, "Be sober, be vigilant, for your adversary the devil walks about as a roaring lion seeking whom he may devour" (1 Peter 5:8).

Yet most children are not able to remain thoroughgoing skeptics forever. From just about every television show they watch and from most every book they read, from their own parents and from most of their teachers, our children are daily bombarded with indefensible dogmas until finally they can withstand the pressure no longer. The lion eventually disappears, and Dorothy leaves the wonders of Oz for the drab plains of Kansas. Fear becomes repressed, and our children give up asking all the important questions. Childhood is massacred and innocence dies. The healthy skepticism of a new generation is vanquished yet again, and adults rest secure in a dogmatic and domesticated universe.

The Skeptic's Last Stand

A militant new dogmatism has taken up arms against the healthy skepticism of ordinary children and ancient pagans, and it has won most of its campaigns. We hate to ask the questions that have haunted us from childhood for fear of seeming foolish, and we keep our doubts and anxieties to ourselves to avoid the danger of appearing old-fashioned or radical or politically incorrect. Skepticism has been defeated.

Yet—and here is the amazing thing—skepticism, though apparently defeated, has not been destroyed. One citadel still remains and in a place we would least expect it. In matters of religion, where dogmatism was once thought to reign supreme, a thoroughgoing skepticism now holds sway. Having been defeated on the open field of battle, our natural skepticism has taken refuge in the abandoned castle of the enemy, where the healthy skepticism of the child and ancient pagan has turned into the cynical skepticism of the modern agnostic.

When it comes to religion in general, and Christian belief in particular, modern dogmatists remain more skeptical than ever. Though they expect their doctor to heal them, the most they expect from prayer is that it may make them feel a little better about being ill. In trying to sort out their personal problems they willingly go to a psychiatrist, but treat priests and ministers as though they have nothing more to offer than personal opinions and private prejudices. When scientists come up with new theories about the universe, these modern dogmatists call it progress, but when a theologian offers some new insight into the nature of God, they see it as an excuse for thinking that all religious belief is just a matter of personal opinion.

The new dogmatist scoffs at the superstition that drove Salem witches to the stake, but avidly reads his horoscope and dabbles in the occult. In tales of science fiction he eagerly pursues the wildest leaps of the imagination as though they might be true, but treats the idea of a virgin birth or bodily resurrection as too wild a fantasy to be entertained. Films like "E.T.", which dramatize the life of Christ under another guise, become box office hits, and the traditional portrayal of the spiritual life in "Snow White and the Seven Dwarfs" becomes a classic. But when it is pointed out that the extraterrestrial being is really the Christ of the Gospels and that the real Prince Charming is the Saviour of the world who overcomes the deadly effect of the seven deadly sins, he continues to dismiss the original gospel stories as so much childish nonsense. Instead, having adopted the dogmatic skepticism of the day, he perversely turns to some fantastic and ill-founded story like "The Last Temptation of Christ" to find out what Christianity is all about.

How We Ended Up Like This

More than two hundred years ago, in the so-called "Age of Enlightenment," religion was shunted onto a siding of fantasy and irrelevance in the ungrounded hope that unaided human reason alone would solve all our problems. But after two centuries of experiment, it has failed to come up with the goods. The more we thought we knew, the more imponderable the universe became, until eventually reason itself was pushed aside by our own irrational feelings.

Faith in scientific reason has turned into an unscientific dogmatism, and the dream of a brave new world into a frightening nightmare. The theoretical scientist has become a mad scientist and the practical scientist a technocrat whose achievements threaten the very life of the planet and perhaps the existence of the whole universe. International attempts to rationalize politics have led to irrational war and violence while planned economies have brought starvation to much of the world. For the individual, analytical psychology has left nervous breakdowns in its train, and battered children are the victims of a rationalized but impersonal social welfare.

The Only Certainty

Yet, with potential destruction all about us, a skeptical age still clings to its old assumptions in the vain hope of finding salvation apart from God. We remain dogmatic about all that is vague and uncertain and unreliable, and only question the one thing we can really be certain about.

Until now most everyone believed that if they were dogmatic about God, they could be skeptical about everything else. They could fearlessly probe the meaning of every personal experience and question every social custom and human institution so long as they did not question the reality of God, for He alone gave them a place to stand from which they might move the world. Today, however, we cling dogmatically to the most outlandish beliefs imaginable because we doubt the only truth that is absolutely true. Because we are no longer dogmatic about God, we continue to fall prey to every popular opinion that comes our way and to seize upon every fad that the hidden forces of consumerism manage to create.

If we are ever to find any worthwhile certainty in our lives, we must learn to become skeptical of our religious skepticism and agnostic about our own ingrained agnosticism.

The Reality of God

We can be certain about the reality of God because God is reality itself.

If I am out walking in the country with my friend on a bright Sunday afternoon and suddenly call out, "Look over there in the next field. Do you see an amazingly fat pig?", my friend likely will follow my gaze in the hope of beholding the wondrous sight of an unusually round pink creature with a cutoff nose at one end and something very much like an over-sized pin curl at the other. Should I however exclaim, "See the beautiful unicorn in the next field," my friend is more likely to gaze into my eyes than into the field, doubting my integrity or my sanity.

Both of us know what a unicorn is and we have a fairly good idea what we mean by a fat pig, but, whereas experience and the stories of others have led us to believe that fat pigs really exist, the claim that a unicorn exists raises a new and astounding idea which goes contrary to all our previous experience and teaching.

It could, of course, be the other way round. I can easily imagine that on this or some other far-flung planet there are fields filled with unicorns but without a fat pig in sight. Search as much as I will, I might be forced to conclude that I live in a universe of unicorns in which fat pigs are nothing more than a rather delightful but eccentric figment of my own imagination. There is, after all, nothing about my idea of fat pigs, or of unicorns for that matter, which requires them to exist. I can imagine that they exist, but by doing so I cannot make them exist.

But even though I dare not be dogmatic about the existence of pigs or unicorns, I have to be dogmatic about the fact that some things do exist, and that even though nothing in particular has to be real, there is such a thing as reality. I must, at the very least, be dogmatic about the reality of a mind that can imagine the existence of unicorns. Even if I should be nothing more than a speck of dust on the floor imagining all this, I must still be dogmatic about the existence of the speck.

I must face the fact that Reality is real, that Existence exists and that Being simply is. On the surface the fact seems a mere truism so obvious as to be hardly worth mentioning. Yet once it is said, we are plunged into realms too profound to be grasped by our small minds and too mysterious to be understood. In such an obvious truism the very mystery of the universe is revealed and the depths of all our experience is probed. By rediscovering the obvious we come face to face with none other than God Himself.

To be dogmatic about the reality of God is simply to be dogmatic about reality itself. Even the old-fashioned atheist understood that much. He at least believed in some kind of reality totally independent of his own ideas, and he desperately wanted to know what it was like. He fought for truth because he passionately believed there was such a thing as truth. It was not reality that the atheist denied but only a previous generation's image of reality. He did not really deny the existence of God but only the God of his forefathers. He did not suffer from a lack of faith but from a generation gap.

A Devotee of the Gods

Today, however, most people neither agree nor disagree with their forefathers because they are no longer interested in the meaning of existence nor in the nature of reality. When little Joey asks why water runs downhill or why trees are green, he is on a spiritual quest, searching into the depths of the mind and heart of God. But when he hears only answers that answer nothing, he abandons his quest and, ceasing to wonder at the mystery behind the appearances of things, the certainty of God dies within him. He loses his natural capacity for wonder and learns to get on with life as best he may. Unlike the former atheist, he does not deny the existence of God but simply loses all interest in the question. He has become a dogmatic skeptic who no longer denies or questions anything at all.

Because today's skeptic does not believe in anything very deeply, he never questions anything very seriously. Having lost interest in God, he falls prey to every god he encounters and to every esoteric fashion that comes along, be it the demonic gods of success and security, or the benevolent but seemingly powerless gods of justice, peace, and general goodwill; be it drugs or transcendental meditation, LSD, or CND, hooliganism, fascism or feminism, vegetarianism or genetic engineering. Any of these may prove good or bad in themselves but he has no way of knowing one way or the other because he has no place where he can take a stand on anything whatsoever. His very doubts about the reality of God have made him a devotee of all the gods.

5

The Power of the Gods

We do not talk much about the gods these days. If you have ever thought about them at all, it was probably when you had to memorize their names for an exam in ancient history. They belonged to the world of myth, rather foolish supernatural fantasies invented by denizens of a more ignorant age. Belief in the gods may have comforted primitive people afraid of the unknown, and fear of the gods may have helped them control others more ignorant than themselves. But ever since we stopped believing in Santa Claus, our teachers have made it clear that all these gods—whatever help they may have been to ancient peoples—were killed off many centuries ago and certainly have no place in the modem mind.

Yet the ancient gods are far from dead and anything but foolish. We have simply failed to recognize them, because ever since we were born, they have been walking through our lives disguised as little more than everyday things and very ordinary people.

May the Force Be with You

You and I cannot possibly remember our original encounter with the gods, because they first showed up when all of us were far too young to remember much of anything. It may have happened when we began to sense that our mothers were potential enemies who might take away our life support system at any time, or perhaps it was when we realized that the bars of our cribs were really prisons designed by some insidious power to curtail our freedom. The gods may have revealed themselves when our legs buckled out from under us and it seemed as though the floor, driven by some sort of perverse hostility, rose up to strike us in the face. But whenever it was, at some such traumatic moment all of us became vaguely aware of innumerable forces impinging upon our lives, forces which the ancient pagans called "the gods" but which today we call nothing at all.

In the womb our every need is met. Aware neither of ourselves nor of anything other than ourselves, we simply exist. But then birth suddenly throws us out into a world quite indifferent to our basic needs. All sorts of objects object to our most innocent desires and seem ready to punish us for the slightest offense. When we are hungry there is no one to feed us, and if we cry in pain we are mere crybabies. Like the people of old we find ourselves face to face with forces that for some unknown reason seem to have it in for us, forces much greater than ourselves, whimsical, arbitrary, and often vindictive forces that need to be conquered or at least controlled.

These forces are none other than the ancient gods, gods that we need to appease or cajole into helping us fulfill our dreams. We must do our best to win them over to our side and perhaps even turn them into friends. With the wise old teacher from *Star Wars* our hearts echo the universal prayer of all humanity: "May the Force be with you."

The Religious Quest

With that semiconscious prayer our religious quest begins, though most of us seldom think of it as particularly religious. Isolated in the midst of an alien world and surrounded by mysterious gods we cannot name, we look yearningly for some sort of peace in an enemy territory and companionship in a hostile land. In one way or another all of us are searching for that deep inner peace common to all religions. We seek that peace which the ancient Jews called "shalom" and the Navaho Indians "hozro," that undifferentiated "nirvana" of the Buddhist where all alienation comes to an end, that perfect balance of "yin" and "yang," sought after by the Chinese, that peace which "passes all understanding" claimed by the faithful Christian.

Once we begin our quest for this mysterious inner peace, we soon discover that not all the gods are hostile. Sometimes we find friendship where we least expect it and love when we need it most. Even as children we soon learn that the grown-ups in our life are not only gods to be

feared but potential friends who, in several ways, are very much like ourselves. As we mature we gradually come to realize that our own parents,
who drew from us a strange combination of awesome respect and genuine affection, are surprisingly much like ourselves, reflecting, like a
many-faceted mirror, the many aspects of our own complex personalities. They think much the way we think, dream dreams like ours, and,
like us, make up their own minds about what they want to do. Soon we
come to the amazing discovery that this is also true of everyone we
know and, to some extent, of everything else as well, whether human or
not.

When I was a child I liked my neighbor's dog because there was
something about him very much like me. He too could run about and
play and obey my commands, just as I had to obey my parents' commands. And as I loved the dog who did my bidding, so I envied the lion
who had more power than I or even than my parents, and I sometimes
wondered what it would have been like to have been born a lion instead
of a little boy. Everything I met was shot through with signs of my own
personality and struck certain cords of recognition within me. Roses
and brussels sprouts showed signs of life I found in myself, the very stars
shone with a glory similar to my own dreams of glory, and rocks and
rivers had a stability and dependability I looked for in myself.

Alienation

Yet there was also something missing in everything around me.
Parents and other grown-ups, no matter how much like me they sometimes seemed, actually lived in a world very different from my own. And
even though my neighbor's dog was in some ways a companion closer to
me than my parents could ever be, I could never converse with him
about my hopes and fears. Though the lion's power was greater than
mine, I also had a power I could never share with him; I could argue to
my heart's content about the rights and wrongs of eating people and he
had no way of answering back. All the animals may be our friends in a
Walt Disney fantasy, but in real life we are alienated from the animal
kingdom, not only from the wild things but even from our dearest pets
in the things that matter most.

What is true of our pets is true of everything else as well. Roses and
sprouts, though alive, can neither sit up and beg for food nor run to us

when we call, and there is no way that stars and stones, with neither breath nor life, intelligence nor freedom, can ever offer us the companionship we so desperately desire. We can kick the stone that skins our knees as often as we like, but it will make absolutely no difference to the stone, for no matter how violent our attack, it neither loves us nor hates us but simply remains a stone.

Stones and stars, sprouts and dogs, fathers and mothers are similar to us in so many different ways, and yet a great gulf exists between them and us which no power on earth can possibly bridge. The peace we seek seems always just beyond our grasp. The companionship we crave is never able to completely pierce the heart of our profound loneliness.

We live in hope that sooner or later we will run into someone who completely understands us and gives us the support we need—a girlfriend or boyfriend perhaps, or a future spouse and child. It may be a teacher or pastor or our best friend. Yet it never turns out quite as we had hoped. We may have a good number of close friends, a very understanding husband or wife, and several loving children, but we soon learn that none of them completely understands us, and that they will most often let us down at those very moments when we need them most. And it's no wonder. They cannot possibly give us all the support we need because they themselves need all the support we can give to them. They are not all-powerful gods but mere human beings like ourselves with the same loves and fears and cares that we have. We ask of them what only real gods can give and the burden is too great for them to bear.

Taming the Gods

Bonds of affection endear us to our families and friends, but wonder and awe drive us to worship the gods. The forces that assault us on every side drive us to our knees because they are greater than we are and beyond our control. Alienated and alone in a world filled with all sorts of mysterious beings, we bow down before them with fear and tremble in humble adoration.

The ancient Egyptians worshiped the sun because they needed the sun in order to live. And the Assyrians worshiped the moon because, as they were quick to point out, the sun shone only when it was light already. To the Greeks and Romans it seemed obvious that the god of the storm, whether they called him Zeus or Jupiter, was king of all the gods and their very lives depended upon his every whim. They treated kings and heroes more powerful than themselves as children of the gods. The pagan soldier at the foot of the cross paid Jesus a great compliment, but he did not experience some sudden conversion when he exclaimed, "Truly this was the son of a god." So, after all, was Caesar.

People may like to think that there is a spark of the divine in every speck of sand and in every child that walks the earth, but even if it were so, our subservient respect and awesome worship will be reserved for the wild animals prowling through the darkness and the capricious volcano towering above us. Far from creating the gods after our own image and likeness, as some philosophers claim, we pay divine honors only to those forces and creatures that are most unlike us and quite indifferent to our needs. We bow down before the neighboring mountain only when we have no idea when it may erupt, and we venerate only those animals we fear may attack at the slightest whim. Once we think we can predict the erratic behavior of the local volcano, or learn how to domesticate the animals roaming in the wild, we no longer worship them as gods but enjoy them as companions existing for our own pleasure or instruments to fulfill our every desire. By turning animals into pets and mountains into package holidays we secularize the sacred and make the world safe for our own private pursuits.

With bloody sacrifices and mysterious incantations, ancient peoples sought peace of mind by attempting to win the gods over to their side. In our own search for peace we try to secularize our alien and frightening world by killing off its hostile gods, living in the hope that eventually—by our own wits and with the help of modern technology—we will bring everything under our control. But in our heart of hearts we know it will never happen. The gods are not so easily domesticated nor so casually destroyed. Demanding our subservient worship they forever remain arbitrary and deceitful, lustful, selfish, and aggressive.

Divine Demands

You may try to avert the wrath of the storm god by planning your life around the predictions of the weather channel, but a surprise downpour can still spoil your picnic or a freak bolt of lightning destroy your house. With myriads of drugs and a variety of therapies, you can try to cajole the god of healing and appease the angel of death. Yet your son still dies of cancer. You worship the god of love only to find that the other gods are jealous and the objects of your devotion betray you.

The gods cannot give you peace because they are themselves at war with one another, competing for our undivided attention and devotion. The demands of conscience, friends, family, church, job, or school all pull us in opposite directions so that to fulfil our commitment to one is to betray one of the others. If you give yourself over to some kind of political idealism, the realities of political life will strike you down. If you devote yourself to your work, your family will feel rejected. But if you put your family first, you are likely to lose your job and the only means you have for supporting them.

How then are we to escape this battleground of competing gods?

6

War Without End

Forces beyond our control assail us on every side. They may be the nameless "they" in Washington or the faceless men and women of the IRS. Or we may give them a name, calling them adverse market conditions or bad luck on the stock exchange, racial minorities, or the neighbor next door. If we are of a more spiritual bent, we may identify them as supernatural demons or the heavy hand of fate. But whatever we call them, in one way or another all of us are engaged in a perpetual battle with potentially hostile gods—gods before whom we bow down in awesome fear and humble adoration. Yet they are gods against whom we must protect ourselves, if we are ever to survive.

Before we ever reached adolescence we developed techniques for keeping hostile gods at bay. We learned magic incantations like "sticks and stones will break my bones but names will never harm me"; we obeyed such simple rituals as never stepping on cracks in the pavement; perhaps we kept a rabbit's foot or some other talisman in our pockets.

Yet these were little more than children's games to prove that we could walk the streets in safety. Throughout the ages adults have invented far more complex weapons to protect themselves against real or imaginary forces beyond their control: sacrificial rites and political power, exotic methods of meditation and scientific research, esoteric art and the pursuit of financial security—to name but a few.

All are valiant attempts to ward off the onslaught of the gods. But ultimately all of them fail. Sacrificial rites develop into grotesque forms of human sacrifice, meditation can turn into drug-induced forms of self-destruction, scientific knowledge and political power become wed in the charred remains of Hiroshima, and artistic imagination is reduced to little more than a source of private wealth feeding an insatiable greed.

Dreams of Glory

Our battle with a hostile world is everlasting and the outcome beyond our control. For it is ultimately a supernatural battle, and one in which we almost always end up the victims. Relief comes only in those rare moments when we are free to indulge in daydreams uninterrupted. In our private dreams of glory we ourselves become the gods of this world, and the awesome and fearful forces assailing us become docile slaves forced to do our bidding. We dream that by sneaking up on the enemy and capturing him unawares, we can make the world safe for ourselves and for our friends—safe for democracy or socialism, for capitalism, atheism, or Buddhism. Safe for whatever idealism happens to strike our fancy.

Years ago, during the Second World War, *The New Yorker* published a series of cartoons called "Dreams of Glory." One that has stayed in my memory was of a small boy standing across from Hitler's desk with a pistol in each hand, crying out in the best John Wayne fashion, "Stick 'em up!" Underneath the cartoon was the caption, "Dreams of Glory." Of such romantic material are those dreams of glory made which drive us forward and give us hope in the midst of personal failure and despair. They offer us a fragile peace and make us feel that the day will come when we may actually conquer the gods.

And a Dream of Terror

But though our dreams of glory may offer us a ray of hope in a hostile world, they can also prove most dangerous. Not only can they distract us from getting on as best we can with the business of living in the "real world" of everyday life, they also never really take away the pain of alienation suffered in that world, but just drive it deeper into the inner recesses of our hearts. Sometimes, when the anxieties of everyday life and the fear of tomorrow become too great, we are tempted to escape down the path of self-destruction, running back to our mother's womb where we can forget ourselves altogether. Or else we try to bury ourselves in some commune of conformity or esoteric spirituality, a kind of impersonal nirvana where nothing makes any difference anymore and nothing can affect us. We give up the battle of everyday life, but in doing so we merely surrender to its gods. This is no strategic retreat or an alternative dream of glory, but rather a dream of terror. In a nightmare of casual indifference and conformity to social pressure, we run the risk of losing our own personal identities forever. By retreating from the battlefield of the gods we endanger our own souls.

As Faust learned when he made a deal with the devil, it is dangerous to make peace with the gods. In bartering with the enemy we end up losing our own humanity, allowing alien forces to pillage our distinctive personality, which is the only thing really worth fighting for. Our supernatural warfare is lost before we even begin to fight, and the enemy returns from the battlefield bearing all the victorious trophies of an unjust war.

Only in the epic dream worlds of Homer or Tolkien do heroes win a final victory over the gods and return to their native lands in peace— Frodo to The Shire and Ulysses back to Ithaca. We would like to think that this is the end of the story and that once we have exposed all the wizards of Oz as frauds, we can cry out with Dorothy, "There's no place like home." But it never turns out this way in real life for, as the film *Star Wars* makes abundantly clear, after the initial victory there is always a sequel. In the tales of all those who have done battle with the gods we learn the bitter truth that every hero is a tragic hero and every victory a Pyrrhic one. With Luke Skywalker we discover that the empire always strikes back. As that great defender of the Christian faith, G.K. Chesterton, once said about the White Horse of the English Berkshire Hills, and about the church and all other things worth keeping, "If you would have the horse of old you must scour the horse anew." In his epic poem celebrating the victories of King Alfred, Chesterton wisely prophesies that when the king grows old and too weak to fight, the barbarians will come again. The unending refrain resounds throughout the ages: "I tell you naught for your comfort, yea naught for your desire, save that the sky grows darker yet and the sea rises higher."

A Victorian Twist

This is the prophetic warning that has rung down the ages. At least, that is, until our Victorian grandparents put a new twist to the old tales. In the dream world of Lewis Carroll's Wonderland everything suddenly became personal, whimsical, and arbitrary except for Alice herself. Rabbits now talk and hatters are mad but she has become a god of hard mathematical fact. Rationalism has won the day and hope now lies in subduing the hostile gods of this world simply through unfeeling reason. By ignoring their own hearts' desires and adjusting their minds to the implacable laws of an impersonal world, our grandparents thought that the world itself could be reduced to their own tyrannical control. A new religion was born in which the scientific method became the only means of salvation. Scientists became the new saints and the abandonment of personal dreams of glory became the new human sacrifice.

The early Fathers of the Christian Church reduced the ancient gods to impotent demons, but the Victorians went a step further and turned them into impersonal objects and mere physical forces. Lightning was no longer king of the gods but only lightning; the stars became mere chunks of matter, and matter itself only bundles of energy to be understood and controlled by science. At long last the gods were dead, having been killed off by nothing more than a Bunsen burner in a chemist's laboratory and the deft stroke of the modern philosopher's pen.

Self-Destruction

Having tasted the blood of battle and with victory over the whole universe seemingly in their grasp, a previous generation did not stop at killing off the gods. They ended up destroying the godlike character of themselves as well.

Writers soon attempted to explain the complexities of human behavior by reducing us to naked apes, casting to one side imagination and will and all those other good things that make us uniquely human. Others taught that our minds were nothing more than electrical impulses of the brain and our brains no different from the mathematical calculations of the computer. In the philosophy of Behaviorism the last vestiges of our freedom were swept away, so that we who set about to control the universe now became relatively insignificant components of a universal machine that ran on its own steam.

In destroying everything that makes us uniquely human, we ended up destroying the reality of just about everything else as well. By trying to rid the world of whatever objects to our desires, we destroyed objectivity itself. All became subjective and a matter of opinion. Nothing was real, nothing good or bad, but feeling could make it so. Objective truth and standards of goodness—as well as the threat of evil—were all brushed aside. Nothing was left for our schools to do but teach us how to express ourselves. Everything unique about us was destroyed, and all that was special and valuable in our world was gradually erased from human consciousness. No longer believing in the gods, we no longer believed in ourselves. An endemic lack of self-confidence became the disease of the day and depression its most devastating symptom.

Because we no longer believe in ourselves we can believe in little else, as we are the only creatures we can know directly and immediately, creatures who dream and worry, make decisions and act for good or ill, who know certain things and know that they know, who feel pain and joy, who laugh and weep, love and hate, feast and dream—creatures capable of being loved or betrayed. Only through the mystery of ourselves are we able to see into the mystery of everything else as well. By coming to know ourselves, we discover the cosmos, and through our godlike qualities we recognize the gods.

If we then declare that the gods are dead, we do little more than kill off our own godlike souls. To will the destruction of the gods must always be our last will and testament, for once the gods have gone nothing more can happen. We may still walk the earth, but we walk as the living dead.

Divine Revenge

This godless and soul-destroying world in which most of us grew up is a mere figment of human imagination. The real world remains exactly the same as always, as alien as ever, and not nearly as godless as we have been led to believe. The ancient gods are far from dead. By denying their existence we do not get rid of them, but rather avert our eyes so that they can go about their business unchallenged and undetected. Like everyone who has ever lived, we enter this world as pagans. But we have been deprived of all the magical rites, religious techniques, and inner resources by which pagans of an earlier time dealt with those powerful gods that today we neither know nor recognize.

Our grandparents thought that by killing off all the gods they would make it possible for us to live our lives without being haunted by the superstitious fears of previous generations. But they have been proven terribly wrong. No longer believing in the gods, the gods have now struck back, and we who thought we had conquered the awesome forces of this world have become the victims of all we thought we had conquered. By trying to force everything in our environment to serve our own ends, the environment itself now threatens to destroy us and all earthly life as we have known it. Victory over alien gods only succeeds in killing off the victors in an alien world where, as the ancient prophet once foretold, the fool alone cries out, "'peace, peace' when there is no peace."

This has been the sad story of the twentieth century. In stripping Germany of all its power after World War I, we succeeded only in giving birth to Hitler. By destroying the gods that ruled the empires of the earth, we have created the tyrants of Cambodia, Uganda, and Iraq. The price we have paid for reducing the gods of ancient myths to unthinking objects and subservient forces within our potential control is the very destruction of the bodies and souls of millions of men and women. And now, in the ultimate attempt to control our own personalities and destinies through genetic engineering, we seem to be preparing ourselves for the end of life on earth as we have known it.

The gods still reign supreme and the world remains our potential enemy, no matter how much we may try to tame it. If, through our economic greed, we destroy all the trees of the Amazon Forest, the tree gods themselves will have their revenge by destroying the whole ecological balance of the planet. Commit the sacrilegious act of polluting the air, and the sky gods will gather up the atmosphere and let it escape through a hole in the ozone layer until eventually there may be no air left for us to breathe. Delve into the very depths of the forces behind all the gods, and "The Force" will strike us down; crack the atom and the earth bursts asunder.

No wonder the heroes of the ancient tales are always tragic heroes. In a world that cannot be controlled by mere mortals or transformed into something other than itself, human life must always end in tragedy. Endurance rather than victory is the most we can hope for in our perpetual battle with the gods. The sensible person must either learn to keep a stiff upper lip with the ancient Stoics, or else join the Epicureans and "eat, drink and be merry, for tomorrow [he] will die."

Postmodernist Angst

Denizens of the "Modern Age" thought they had killed off all the gods or at least made them completely impotent, but we are postmodernists who have discovered that we still live in a mysterious universe beyond our control. Rediscovering the reality of the gods, a new generation is now searching for new religious techniques and new religious fervor to help them engage in supernatural warfare. Hoping to overcome the gods of the established order, some hand themselves over to different forms of satanic worship, only to be taken over by forces of evil beyond their control. Eventually they too have to learn that the gods are no more easily removed from their thrones by the worship of evil than by the pursuit of good.

Others try to create a cultural revolution by adopting the esoteric life of one of the new religion cults, without realizing that revolutionaries are always defeated by the religious fervor of their own revolutions. Religious fervor may be necessary in fighting the gods, but it will not help us avoid the mortal wounds of combat. And it can prove very dangerous, as we discovered at the end of the seventies when, in obedience to a self-proclaimed messiah, a thousand people marched off to Ghana and drank from a vat of cyanide, only to be followed by close to a hundred others going to their deaths in Waco.

Our attempt to find peace and harmony in this world may at times have a certain tragic nobility about it, but it must eventually end in failure. We may travel to the outermost star and make the forces of the cosmos do our bidding. Closer to home we may learn to prune the roses, tame the lion, and domesticate the neighbor's dog. Yet we can never ultimately resolve our fundamental conflict with warring gods who will continue to do battle with the likes of us long after we are gone.

The everlasting warfare goes on, no matter what any of us try to do about it. If you join the war you will end up the loser, and if you remain outside the fray you will become an innocent victim. To escape such certain defeat you may try to run away from the conflict altogether by retreating into yourself or by burying yourself in your work or perhaps by declaring yourself an atheist. But there is no such easy escape from the gods; simply pretending that they are not there cannot destroy them nor drive them away.

Perhaps the ancient philosophers were right when they saw this earthly body as a prison house from which our eternal soul has to escape. But, if so, then the only escape is death, and nobility will be found only in suicide, honor in self-destruction, and peace in the obliteration of our own unique individuality.

Like St. Paul we cry out, "Who will deliver us from this death?"

Part II

Surprised by God

7

Born to Be Jews

If you and I are to be delivered from spiritual death, we must some-how learn to rise above all the pressures and forces competing for our allegiance, those warring forces which the ancients once called the gods. We must find a place to stand in the shifting sands of our own inner turmoil. If we are to have any kind of peace in ourselves and the world in which we live, we must search for some kind of god who will care for us and yet remain unscathed by the conflicting forces of this world, a unique god to whom we can sacrifice ourselves without losing our own integrity.

But among the vast array of philosophies and religions scattered throughout the world, how are we to find such a god? Should we become Platonists, Marxists, or Moonies, Buddhists, Moslems, or Mormons? Perhaps we should join forces with the Baptists, Presbyterians, or Catholics. With so many vendors promoting their spiritual wares, it seems rather as though we are simply jumping from the frying pan of competing gods into the fire of competing religions, with no clue as to which one we should follow.

Choosing among them may seem hopelessly difficult. Yet it is not that impossible, for there is really very little to choose from. With one notable exception the world's religions are only variations on a single theme. As with the ancient pagans, they all still treat the world as some-thing divine, in which the gods remain the personified forces of every-day life. They differ only in the techniques they offer for escaping from life's chaos, pain, and turmoil. Platonists offer an intellectual escape, Buddhists and Christian Scientists try to escape into pure spirit, and militant capitalists and Marxists deny spiritual reality for the peace of an egalitarian society and materialistic prosperity.

People have generally assumed that if they dig deep enough they will find the key to their salvation somewhere in this world. Others, however, insist that only by despising this world will we ever be saved from the warfare of its competing gods. We are left then with only two choices: We can stand with those who affirm the virtues of this world or with those who deny them.

Most religions and philosophies fall into one of these two camps— but not quite all. A few of them build all their beliefs and practices upon the assumption that at the heart of our individual experience there is another God above all the gods, a God who is outside our world, yet who made the world out of nothing and proclaims that it is very good. They worship a God who reigns supreme over all the forces dominating our lives, a God who doesn't get enmeshed in the never-ending warfare of lesser beings.

Out of This World

The beliefs and practices of Judaism, Christianity, and Islam stand apart from all other philosophies and religions. All three derive from a single ancient tribe of Near Eastern nomads who wandered around the Sinai desert almost 4,000 years ago. They alone believed in a God who actually cares about what happens to us and to our world but who is not affected by its unceasing warfare. From these ancient Jews we learn of a God we can revere without falling into the pagan trap of investing the world with divine personalities vying with one another for the ultimate control of our souls.

From what we can tell, the Jews started off no different from the rest of us. Like you and me, they grew up with objects that objected to their own desires and with things and people that seemed to hold mastery over their lives. Unlike their devout pagan neighbors, however, they did not search for peace in the midst of these warring gods as it never occurred to them that the people and things with which they had to come to terms were actually divine. In this they were like the modern secularist. But unlike the secularist, they did not leave it at that. Behind the arbitrary catastrophes of daily life and all the fiery darts of outrageous fortune, behind the cold and indifferent fate that so often seems to rule our lives, these ancient Jews insisted that there is one Lord and Master of the universe, and that peace is to be found only in obeying His will. The true God is above, beyond, and outside all the conflicts of this world; He overrides or transcends our everyday experience and remains true to Himself in spite of every earthly trial. These Jews, like all who have followed in their footsteps, believed they were safe from the warring gods of this world because a God who is not of this world had saved them. As the Jewish Prayer Book always insisted, heaven is God's throne and earth is His footstool: "He dwells between the cherubim, be the earth never so unquiet."

Because their God was not a God of arbitrary whim, the Jews believed that they could depend upon Him to save them from the warring gods of this world. He knows His own mind. He is consistent in everything He does because He is at one with Himself. There is nothing schizophrenic about Him, no stresses nor strains within Him. Because He is not at war with Himself they could count on Him to do whatever He said.

Order and Disorder

The Jews believed that the true God was a God of law and order who had built order into the world He had made. In spite of all the changes and chances of life, they could trust the world to behave in an orderly and predictable way. The Jew did not find the presence of God in the occasional miracle so much as in the dependability of cause and effect. As the Jewish psalmist proclaimed, and the ancient pagan never understood: "He made the round world so sure that it cannot be moved at any time." Plague, fire, and famine might be signs of God's anger, but He is more clearly seen in the daily rising of the sun.

The Jews believed that laws ordained by God ran the universe. Breaking them led to inevitable disaster. Yet break them they did and, in doing so, they found the key to unlock the mystery of their own humanity. They learned that they could sin. No longer could they blame all the disasters of life on the whims of arbitrary gods. Human tragedy did not come from trying to compete with gods more powerful than themselves, nor from making mistakes, nor from breaking taboos, but from living a disorderly life in an orderly world. The Jew could choose to be an enemy of God, but by doing so he only ended up becoming his own worst enemy. Or he could obey God and be at one with the world around him. The choice was his. By following God's orders he could maintain order in his own life and enjoy something of that inner peace we are all looking for, that "shalom" which the Jew found in the tranquility of order.

The Smashing of Idols

By obeying God's laws the Jews discovered that they had a place to stand above the quicksand of pagan doubt and despair. They could stand back and look more objectively at all the mysterious and terrifying forces playing havoc with their lives, and in doing so they found that these mysterious forces were not as terrifying as they had originally thought. By worshiping the Master of the Universe, the universe itself paled into relative insignificance and the shackles of religious devotion fell away from all created things. Before the God of the Jews the river gods fled, the sky gods retreated into the heavens, every other god turned to dust, and Mother Nature became truly natural for the first time. So long as they focused their devotion elsewhere, the heavens and the earth were free to be themselves rather than a pantheon of supernatural gods vying for our allegiance. Now the Jews and their spiritual descendants could begin to use earthly things for their own enjoyment because they no longer worshiped them as idols. And they no longer had to worship kings or presidents as though they were gods. They could also begin to treat women and little children as real human beings; they no longer had to pretend that they were goddesses or little angels.

Images of God

If you start looking at the world through the eyes of the ancient Jews, you will find that it is rather like looking through the wrong end of a telescope. The powers that once governed our lives become clearer and more distinct than ever before, but smaller and less significant. Because people and things—though they all reflect something of God's glory—are no longer gods, we can appreciate them for their real worth without having to make demands on them that they cannot possibly fulfill. By worshiping a God above all the gods, we are able to adore our husbands and wives as they really are because we do not have to place them on some sort of divine pedestal. We can train, cherish, and protect our children as real children with distinct personalities, instead of trying to fit them into our own image of what we think they ought to be. In spite of having to change their diapers and seeing that they do not swallow the bottle of aspirins or step on the dog's tail, we know that even as babies they are made in the image of God and, because God is completely personal, they are capable of becoming complete persons as well. We even dare to pray that some-day our children may become like God, but only if we realize that we dare not treat them as gods the way they are right now.

By believing that they, along with husbands and wives and neigh-bors, have all come from God, the ancient Jews could see the image of God in everyone, much as we first discovered helium here on earth.

With the aid of a spectroscope scientists originally found this mys-terious element in the sun, and then, believing that the earth came from the sun, they looked for it closer to home, eventually finding it lurking in the caves and dens of the earth. In much the same way the Jews were able to find unexpected signs of the wonder and glory of God lurking even in the deep recesses of their children's souls. Yet it would never have occurred to them to look for these intimations of divine glory in such unlikely places if they had not already seen something of the wonder and glory of God Himself.

If we had been born old-fashioned Jews, we would have honored our children for what they might become, insisting with the psalmist that God created them a little lower than the angels to crown them with glory and honor. Unlike the pagans we would not have placed them on the burning pyres of human sacrifice. Neither would we have thrown those we did not want over the cliffs into the sea in the manner of the ancient Greeks. Nor would we have sent them floating down the sewers of ancient Rome. Nor for that matter would we have aborted them as we do today, no matter how awkward or inconvenient their births might be.

As the ancient Jews could love their children for what they might become, so they could honor their parents for showing them something of what God is like. They could appreciate their fathers as a faint image of God Himself once they came to accept God as their real Father. They did not have to despise their natural fathers for squandering all the shopping money on drink nor hate them for beating up their mothers when they came home drunk at night. In spite of the sins of their natu-ral fathers, they could also enjoy occasional glimpses of a wisdom and justice and mercy that fit in with what they had come to know about

God Himself. By calling God Father, they were not really saying much about God at all, but were saying a great deal about what human fathers should be like.

Our Jewish Inheritance

In the very depths of our psyches we are all Jews. Ancient Jewish attitudes are part of our own mental furniture; they provide the dogmatic structure of our lives. Like it or not, all of us have been brought up to think like Jews and we all have a Jewish way of looking at things, even if we never thought of it as particularly Jewish.

For myself I find that these attitudes and the beliefs on which they were originally built make sense. They fit my experience and satisfy a deep yearning within me. And this may be true of you as well. Like me, you may find that they liberate you from slavery to your own passions and give direction and purpose to your life. By consciously accepting the God of the Jews in which you were raised, you may discover for the first time a new sense of inner peace, no matter what personal trials and tragedies may come your way.

Yet you and I are not inevitably tied to these beliefs. Just as the Jew could always reject His God, so you can reject the God of the Jews if you so wish. You can choose to join that diminishing group of atheists instead. In fact, it is only because you and I have been brought up with a Jewish mindset that we are free to be atheists. We can deny the reality of God only because we have been taught to believe in the kind of God who can be denied.

Pagans do not doubt the existence of the gods because they almost never think about the gods. They experience them, and there is no way anyone can consciously deny his own experience. But the Jew believed he was told about God, and everyone is free to disbelieve what he is told. Only Jews, and those who have been brought up with a Jewish mindset, can deny their Jewish inheritance. Only those with the faith of a Jew are free to deny the faith.

You may decide not to believe in God, but it is only the God of the Jews that you will decide not to believe in, for you are a child of Abraham if only by adoption. You and I can think in no other terms and know of no other gods. We are not able to worship new gods of our own making, no matter how much we try, because we always know that they are of our own making.

The Loss of Pagan Virginity

Today we are buffeted about by all sorts of forces and objects that the ancients worshiped as gods, and we are still caught up in their everlasting warfare. They are as real as ever, but we can no longer worship them or even give them a name. Because we are no longer pagans, most of us rarely even recognize the ancient gods. Much like a woman who divorces her husband, we may reject the God of our Jewish inheritance but we can never again regain our pagan virginity.

From time to time small groups of people try to resurrect the old pagan gods, like those who gather in England every year to perform their Rites of Spring at Stonehenge in imitation of ancient druids, or like Anglos in the United States who imitate the rituals of native Americans. But these esoteric worshipers can never quite bring it off. The ancient druids, like the early Native Americans, were, after all, natural pagans who never tried to be anything other than themselves, whereas their modern imitators are only dissatisfied secularists desperately trying to be something other than themselves. They fail to realize that none of us can deny our cultural inheritance, even if we deny the faith upon which that inheritance has been built.

We are not pagans but spiritual Jews, whether we like it or not. After 4,000 years our culture has been permeated through and through with the Jewish understanding of God, so that by now you and I really have only two choices. Either we believe in the God of the Jews or else we become out-and-out secularists who believe in nothing at all, not even ourselves.

I know which one I would choose. I would much rather believe in the God of the Jews than believe in nothing at all. Yet, the question must still be asked. Do any of us have the right to make such a choice? Just because we have been raised to think that there is a just, loving, and caring God beyond this world of conflict and turmoil does not mean our thinking is necessarily right. Before we can consciously believe in the God of the Jews, we must have some firm evidence that there really is such a God.

And here the ancient Jews are of very little help.

8

Public Relevations

The ancient Jews were never much good at defending their beliefs, whether by scientific experiment or logical argument. They did not produce even a first-rate philosopher until late in their history. I suppose you could call their respect for the laws of cause and effect scientific, but when it came to their belief in God they were about as unscientific as you can get.

They simply insisted that God had personally revealed Himself to them in ways they could not possibly prove by any kind of earthly evidence. If you had asked an Old Testament Jew how he had learned about God, he would have said that God had told him. "Thus says the Lord" was the Jews' constant refrain.

Belief in some sort of personal revelation may have been good enough for these ancient Jews, but it is not likely to be of much use for people like you and me. Few of us are prepared to stake our lives on a faith we have learned about only through hearsay, even if the Jews claim that it is *divine* hearsay. Such blind faith offends the modern mind and flies in the face of all our training. Just as you would almost certainly rebel against anyone who tried to make you accept what they say simply because they say it, or believe what they believe just because they believe it, so you are almost certain to turn a deaf ear to anyone who asks you to accept what God says simply because some ancient people once claimed that He said it. Just as Scrooge thought that Marley's ghost may have been nothing other than a bit of undigested beef, so for all we know the Word of the Lord may have been nothing more than a pathological ringing in the Jewish ear.

On the other hand, if God really is personal it is very hard to see how we could possibly know anything about Him unless he revealed Himself to us in a personal way.

Personal Revelations

We do not believe in our friends through scientific analysis or philosophical speculation. We know them through their autobiographies. Our faith in them depends upon what they choose to reveal about themselves. Written or unwritten, the story of their lives gives us our only authentic insight into their real character and personality.

I suppose that someone could point to all sorts of evidence that my wife is a thief and a liar. Yet I ignore what they say because I know from living with her over a period of years that she is not that sort of a person. I believe in her because I have chosen to believe in her. But this is not an arbitrary choice nor wishful thinking on my part. It is based on a close and intimate relationship that has taught me she can be trusted in spite of anything people may say against her. She has revealed herself to me, and if others wonder what she is really like, they must either take my word for it or else come to know her as I do.

I find that I am constantly placing this same kind of faith in other people, even though there is no clear reason for doing so. The cynic, if he so wishes, can quite easily demonstrate that several people are out to kill me. He may point out that some of my closest friends talk behind my back and others keep poison in the garden shed. Just the other day a friend asked me to climb a ladder from which I could easily have fallen and broken my neck. Yet, in spite of all this damning evidence, I do not go about fearing for my life. I am saved from being paranoid because I realize that most people do not know me well enough to care whether I am dead or alive, and those few who do know me that well seem quite content to let me go on living. I cannot prove scientifically that they are not out to kill me and, indeed, I can think of many reasons why they might, but the better I come to know them the harder it is to think that murder is really on their minds.

I cannot say as much for trees and stones. From what I can tell, stones are extremely callous about my welfare, and as for trees, the only reason it never occurs to me that murder might be on their minds is that they seem so remarkably mindless. The law of averages assures me that most trees are not going to fall in my path and strike me dead, though I still walk somewhat warily through the woods knowing that at any moment one of them might accidentally do so. But if I meet a friend while walking in the woods, we walk together with complete confidence in one another, because—for some strange reason beyond my comprehension—I know that my friends do not wish my immediate demise. Even though I do not deserve it, they really do seem to care for me. In fact, it is precisely because there is no earthly reason why they have to care for me, that—unlike stones and trees—my friends reveal themselves as free and caring people with minds and wills of their own.

Sharing a Personal Faith

This is what the Jews thought about God. They did not suffer from pagan paranoia because they did not think that God was out to get them, even though they often thought they deserved it. Neither was God callous like a stone nor mindless like a tree. Instead, God had revealed Himself as a caring sort of person who, throughout their history, had never betrayed them even though they had often betrayed Him. In their history God had remained faithful, and by doing so He had given the Jews their faith.

We can share this faith, either by accepting what the Jews once said about God or by coming to know God in the same way a modern Jew comes to know Him—not through some philosophical or theological speculation but from hearing the stories of his ancestors. Going to the synagogue every Friday evening, the young Jewish child hears from his father's bank manager or perhaps from the neighborhood grocer the stories of Abraham, the father of his own nation. He learns of Moses, the mediator between God and man whom God called to bring freedom to the Jewish slaves in Egypt and to whom He revealed His will for the people He loved.

The Mystery of Human History

Soon he realizes that his ancestors, like everyone else, started off assuming that there were all sorts of gods competing with one another for their allegiance, the most powerful being the god of the storm and the god of the volcano. Just as the Greeks worshiped Zeus and the Romans worshiped Jupiter, so the Jews worshiped the same god under still another name, a god of cosmic power who became jealous if his people gave too much attention to lesser gods. But then, unlike the peoples around them, they slowly hammered out on the anvil of their common experience a new unique insight into the mystery of divinity.

Then something happened which shook the Jewish nation to its foundations and left an indelible mark on every Jew from that day to this. Something forced the Jews to realize that their own national god was not jealous because he was in competition with other gods, but because he cared for them much too much to let any other god lead them astray.

Intimations of Divine Love

They first began to think that their god really cared for them when Abraham claimed that god had called him out of his native town of Ur of the Chaldees to become the father of a great nation. It was as though, for some mysterious reason, their national god had a special interest in Abraham and his children. For a while this was born out by all the victories they won against neighboring hostile tribes, before finally giving up their nomadic life and settling down in a land they could call their own.

Then something went terribly wrong. Famine struck and they ended up in Egypt where they eventually became the persecuted slaves of Pharaoh. It appeared as though their god had abandoned them to the arbitrary whim of a foreign power beyond their control.

But when all hope seemed lost, Moses rose up out of the Nile to act as a go-between or mediator between the Jews and their god. Under his guidance, this god led the people out of Egypt and rescued them from certain death at the hands of Pharaoh's army. Fleeing the pursuing Egyptians, they were saved from total destruction when the waters of the nearby marshes—lying as a barrier between themselves and their future homeland—were blown aside by a strong east wind, allowing them to cross in safety. Even so, their final deliverance had not yet come, for when they looked back they saw to their horror the Egyptians relentlessly continuing their pursuit through the once watery marshes. They knew that only their god could save them now, but little did they expect him to do precisely that. As they were staring at the Egyptian soldiers desperately trying to dislodge their chariot wheels from the soft mud of the sea bed which they themselves had crossed just moments before, the wind suddenly died down and the enemy drowned in the rush of returning waters.

A God Worthy to Be Called GOD

In such spectacular fashion they learned that their god reigned supreme over all the pagan gods. The tyrannical Egyptians perished in the quicksand of their pagan minds and the one true god led His chosen people—with a cloud during the day and a pillar of fire at night—through the wilderness of trials and temptations towards the Promised Land.

Why the waters fled and what this fire and cloud may have been never much interested the Jews. For them the important thing was that their escape from slavery into freedom brought with it an amazing discovery. Because of this apparently miraculous deliverance, the Jews came to believe that they worshiped the most powerful of all the gods. No longer some sort of personified force arbitrarily controlling their lives, their god had become a real person more powerful than all the forces of this world combined. Able to drive out the mighty gods of the Egyptians, their god alone turned out to be the one and only God, and for some inexplicable reason this personal and all-powerful God had a personal interest in them.

Marching forward in this conviction they won victory after victory over all the nations surrounding them, and later over the powerful Greeks and Syrians who tried to drive them out of the land they believed God had given them. Their victories seemed to prove that "The Force" was personally interested in them and would save them from all the conflicting forces of pagan neighbors. God was on their side and would protect them from the onslaught of the gods.

The Law That Saves

It was then they learned that God was a God of Law and Order, and that you do not play around with such a God unless you know the rules of the game. After saving them from slavery in Egypt and leading them into the wilderness of temptation, God actually revealed his laws to Moses. High upon the mountain, in the midst of lightning, fire, and resounding thunder, God declared His mind, and the people learned that it is a fearful thing to fall into the hands of a living God who is also a God of unchanging and immutable law. This was no Sunday school lesson about decency and respectability but a terrifying experience that shook the Jews to the very depths of their souls. Yet they were forever grateful because the law also saved them from certain death and final destruction.

The Jews saw the law as a special blessing. Knowledge of the law made it possible for them to know what to do and what to avoid, just as knowledge of the law of gravity keeps us from jumping out of windows in the upper floors of office buildings. If we knew nothing about the law of gravity, we would have no fear of open windows and with smiling equanimity quite easily face up to anyone trying to push us out of one. But despite this blissful ignorance, we would still go down instead of up, probably to our certain death. Like the Jews of old, we rarely, if ever, curse the day we came to know the law, for though our knowledge of the law puts serious constraints upon our freedom it also saves our lives.

The Jews believed that in an orderly world some law governs everything that happens, and that only by respecting these laws would everything be all right. By honoring your father and mother and not going about killing your fellow Jews, your national energies would not be dissipated in blood feuds with your neighbors nor would your soldiers betray one another on the battlefield. And if you carefully cleansed all your pots and pans and avoided eating contaminated pork, your soldiers would not be constantly dropping dead from food poisoning. Most important of all, you would have something worth fighting for if you maintained your cultural identity by not getting mixed up with foreigners. You would save the soul of the nation by not marrying the daughters of aliens, nor worshiping their gods, nor eating their strange exotic foods.

It was not the Afro-Americans of the 1960s but the Jews of thousands of years before who first discovered "soul food." And in discovering this soul food, or "kosher" as they called it, the Jews discovered and maintained their cultural identity. Along with all the other laws governing their everyday lives, they also discovered that they could rebel against that identity. They were free to go against the divine laws and eat foreign food if they so wished. They could become "Uncle Toms," betraying their cultural inheritance and going against their God.

Because they knew the law, they also knew how to break the law. By tasting the tree of the knowledge of good and evil, they could become as gods, but only by betraying their national identity and their God.

The Divine Autobiography

To this very day, when a devout Jewish boy hears how God saved his people from slavery in Egypt, his heart wells up within him, not out of nostalgia for an ancient story, but because the ancient story is so very modern. God's salvation of his people was not just a one-time event, but an event that continues throughout the ages. Because God is consistent in everything He does, the devout Jew believes that if He saved His people once He will save them always. Because He once led His people into the Promised Land after years of persecution in Egypt, they could expect Him to lead them into a new State of Israel after the Holocaust of the Second World War. If, at the beginning, He created the world in six days, we need not be surprised that in the 1960s He recreated His people's freedom from Egypt in a Six Day War.

These stories give a Jewish child his national inheritance and make him think like a Jew, whether consciously or not, much like the rest of us came to think like Americans. We learned American ideals and values by hearing stories about George Washington, the father of our country who never told a lie, and about Abraham Lincoln, the mediator who brought freedom to the American slaves. Yet the two are not quite the same. In all the American stories the local heroes are the chief actors, whereas in the Jewish stories the chief actor is God. Acting in the drama of His people's history, He reveals what He likes and what He is like.

Divine revelation is God's autobiography written into the pages of Jewish history.

Becoming Spiritual Jews

What the modern Jew learns in the synagogue, children of Christian families learn in church or in Sunday school. Here you learned about the God of the Jews and about law and order and sin. Even if you never went to church or Sunday school, you were bound to pick up from school and your neighbors many of the ideas and values that were instilled there.

From the stories, wherever we learned them, we all came to think like Jews. Those slaves in Egypt are our own ancestors, and in freeing them from tyranny God makes it clear just what He wants the world to be like. We take it for granted that He has established certain laws for running the world, and we assume that, come what may, if we obey these laws everything will turn out all right, good will overcome evil, and the righteous will win the day by doing what is right. Having been raised spiritual Jews we believe that every story should have a happy ending and that, if we are good little girls and boys and do what we are told, we will live happily ever after and not be thrown on the rubbish heap of the world's disasters.

Most of us take all of this pretty much for granted. We unwittingly accept the Jewish faith without argument or proof. And yet this is not the blind faith once described by Mark Twain, as "believing what you know ain't so." Far from it. Just as my faith in my wife's honesty is based upon my personal experience of her, so the personal faith we have inherited from the Jews can also be tested by personal experience.

Logic demands that if anything exists, some sort of god or gods must exist, but only you can decide to put your faith in a personal God who is said to care for you. Ultimately the faith of the Jew is a moral choice only you can make. No one can make it for you any more than someone else can convince you that you ought to trust your wife. The most anyone can do is point the way, retell the age-old story and invite you to "taste and see that the Lord is good" (Psalm 34:8).

9

Pain and Grief

It is no good me telling you to "taste and see that the Lord is good" when you are standing at the side of a hospital bed watching your son die of cancer. You taste nothing but bitterness and feel only anger and indescribable pain, frustration, helplessness, and a sense of terrible injustice. It is as though part of your very self is dying within you. You feel only half the person you once were, and wonder how much more can be taken from you before there is nothing left at all. "Why," you cry out, "is God doing all this to me? Surely I've never done anything bad enough to deserve all this pain and grief." And, of course, you are right. Life is terribly unfair, and it does no good pretending otherwise. So, if God is to have an important place in these unfair lives of ours, He must first of all respond to the emptiness of our broken hearts.

The Sanity of Suicide

And how does God respond? Not very well, it would seem. You turn to Him for help and He pays you back by letting your son die of cancer. You glance through the pages of history to see God's goodness vindicated, and instead you find the twisted bodies of six million of His chosen people massacred in Nazi gas chambers. You look at His church, and instead of a community of love, you find a holy club more interested in proclaiming their own righteousness than in caring for you. In desperation you give up all hope of finding any kind of supernatural love and look for signs of purely natural affection, only to find thousands of children sexually molested and physically tortured by their parents. You look to your family for support and soon learn that everyone is much too busy with their own affairs to pay any attention to you. Even your closest friends abandon you without reason or suddenly turn and stab you in the back.

Painfully you learn that it is not only death that destroys but betrayal. In a world where no one seems to care about anyone except themselves, there appears to be neither justice nor faithfulness.

This probing into the darkness of pain and grief may be too depressing for those who spend their days whistling in the darkness of the world's disasters, but in our search for God you and I need to see things as they really are. And when we do, signs of God's goodness are far from clear. Given all the pain and grief about us, perhaps we should treat clinical depression as a sign of health rather than a disease. Contrary to the wisdom of the ages, perhaps those who have the courage to kill themselves are our real martyrs, and the world's suicides the only ones who know what life is all about.

Disappointed Expectations

But before we slit our wrists or put a gun to our heads, we need to find out what it is about pain and grief that so depresses us. A life of poverty, as hard as it is, does not in itself make the poor depressed; many are quite happy until they get an idea of what money could buy if only they were rich. There was even a time when people managed quite well without television, but now the breakdown of the television set with children at home is an indescribable tragedy. And have you noticed that when someone who is your enemy stabs you in the back, you are much more likely to get angry than depressed? The pain and grief we all suffer when something goes wrong can actually goad us into action. A stab in the back depresses us only when done by someone we always thought was our friend.

When we are let down by someone close to us, or someone we trust and respect disappoints us, or when the car breaks down just when we need it the most, when we are suddenly deprived of our rights or come up against injustice where we least expected it, it is then we begin to feel that something terribly evil is happening to us. The injustice of it all is what depresses us.

The Problem of Evil

If we thought our sense of justice was only a creation of our own imagination or a cruel joke written into our psyches by whimsical gods,

we would be irritated but not depressed. Nor would pain and grief disturb our faith in God. They never made the ancient pagans doubt their
faith in the gods because they never believed in the goodness of the gods
in the first place. It never occurred to them, any more than it occurs to
the modern cynic, that the forces governing the universe are either good
or bad. They are just very inconvenient at times. In the face of cosmic
cruelty, it seems that the only sane philosophy is to eat, drink, and be
merry for tomorrow everyone will die.

But you and I cannot take cosmic cruelty so casually. Being raised
spiritual Jews we cannot rid our minds of the belief that somewhere out
there must be some kind of real justice. We feel it in our bones and
believe it in our hearts, and when things go wrong our sense of justice
keeps us awake at night and wears us down during the day. We keep
asking what kind of justice allows innocent babies to be tortured. We
have been taught to place our faith in a God of justice, and every time a
child dies that faith comes under attack. We are horrified by evil because
we have grown up placing our faith in divine goodness.

Why Doesn't God Do Something?

Gangs of criminals do not go around worrying about the problem of
crime, nor do drug addicts worry about the drug problem. Crime for them
is normal and drugs a way of life. If, however, they are converted from
their life of crime or try to overcome their drug addiction, then the existence of crime and drugs becomes a real problem for the first time and,
likely as not, they will talk of little else. They crusade against crime. They
devote their lives to rehabilitating other drug addicts. They organize campaigns to wipe out these evils from our social life. Having come to believe
that it is good to live in an honest society of clearheaded people, they do
everything they can to stamp out whatever evil tries to destroy it.

Unless you are yourself a converted criminal or a former drug
addict, you will undoubtedly lack some of their zeal in trying to rid the
world of these evils. Nevertheless, most of us would do our best to wipe
out crime and drug addiction if we had the means and opportunity. And
if we were God, we would never allow hurricanes to destroy whole vil-
lages in Honduras or earthquakes to kill little children in Turkey. We
would rid the world of debilitating diseases, children's deformities, and
every other agony that afflicts the human race. Yet God, who supposedly

could do something about all these evils, doesn't seem to bother. It is as though he is not as good as converted gangs of criminals, or is no more able to rid the world of evil than we are.

There seems to be a devastating contradiction built into the very fabric of the universe. We believe that pain and grief are evil because they go against divine goodness. If, after all, there is no God looking after us out of the goodness of His heart, then what we call evil is really nothing more than personal unpleasantness and we might as well get on with life as best we can. But if there is a God reigning supreme over the whole world, then the very existence of evil makes us doubt His goodness. All the evil in the world goes against everything we have come to believe about Him.

Here then is our dilemma: How can we possibly believe in a God who either has no conscience when it comes to evil or who is too weak to obey what little conscience He has?

Hearing from Others

We are hardly the first people to notice this apparent contradiction between the world's evil and divine goodness. And throughout the centuries people have been trying to come up with some kind of satisfactory solution.

The ancient Jews wrote about the problem of evil in the book of Job, and the answer they came up with was that God was too mysterious and too powerful for us to question what He does. But far from this being a real answer, it simply says that we should not have asked the question. You and I may well wonder how we can put our faith and confidence in a God we are not allowed to question.

Some people have claimed that because we are all so evil, we only get what we deserve, and that, far from complaining about our pain and grief, we ought to thank God our life isn't worse than it is. Yet this won't do either, for though you and I may deserve everything that comes our way, an innocent child certainly doesn't deserve to be tortured by his parents. Nor did six million Jews deserve the gas chambers any more than their German persecutors.

Others agree that life is not very fair but they try to reassure us by claiming we will all get our just rewards in heaven. And for all I know they may be right, but it does not explain why God made life on earth so very unfair in the first place.

Professional theologians try to solve the problem by talking of such things as God's "active will" and His "permissive will," claiming that God does not want little children tortured, but in order to bring about some greater good He allows it to happen. But, I ask myself, what could possibly be good enough to excuse the torture of little children?

The Answer of the Heart

You are not going to find the answer to the world's evils in the dusty tomes of theologians but only by knowing your own heart. There alone will you find a point to all your suffering, and get an inkling as to how it is a part of the mystery of God's goodness rather than its contradiction.

When you examine your own heart, the first thing to notice is the striking difference between your own personal suffering and the suffering of others.

There is only the difference of one letter between a telegram that says "Our son is dead" and one that says "Your son is dead," but this one letter makes all the difference in the world. The first rouses our sympathies but does not necessarily call God into question. Only when something terrible happens directly to us do we begin to doubt our faith. It is as though the only real evil in the world is the evil we feel in ourselves. And in a sense this is true, for it is only when we suffer personally that suffering becomes something depressingly evil.

There are times, of course, when the suffering of others horrifies us almost as much as our own. This is only, however, because we are able to feel in ourselves what the others feel and make their suffering our suffering as well.

We can watch a James Bond film in which people are stabbed or poisoned or blown up and never feel the least twinge of pain or grief about their fate. But let something similar happen to real people on September 11th and we feel their own suffering in ourselves. In moments of horrific suffering, our imagination creates a sort of mysterious exchange of pain between ourselves and others which, at times, can become almost unbearable.

Sympathetic Pain

If we felt the suffering of the whole world at any given moment, we would all go mad. We keep our sanity only because a protective insensitivity keeps us from being infected by other people's pain, and helps us bear the pain that comes our way.

Sometimes we find it very difficult to distinguish between the atrocities pictured on the ten o'clock news and those we see in a James Bond film. One seems as unreal as the other because our built-in defenses protect us from feeling all the unbearable sufferings of people in the news. And this insensitivity must surely be a sign of emotional health and a prerequisite for mental stability

Yet strangely enough, most people do not see it this way. Instead they act as though there is something terribly wrong with us if we are insensitive towards other people's sufferings. Even at the risk of shattering our own peace of mind, others seem to think that it is only right to grieve over other people's suffering and feel something of their pain within our own hearts.

Most of us agree that, in spite of our protective defenses, we ought to feel other people's pain. When we see the agonized faces of tragedy's victims—families of those lost in the twin towers, the poor made homeless by devastating floods, mourners standing round the mutilated bodies of earthquake victims—we feel that our hearts ought to break along with theirs. Few people, if any, blame Mother Theresa for identifying with the sufferings of the poor of Calcutta, but instead seem to think that her expressions of extreme love for the helpless were something we should all try to emulate. Should our own hearts break over the suffering of others, people are more likely to praise than to blame us, even though our broken hearts would only add to the weight of the world's pain.

Here is a strange paradox—that we believe it is a good thing to take upon our own shoulders the sufferings of other people, but should at all costs avoid bringing any suffering upon ourselves. If we feel the pain others feel, we are paraded as saints, but if we inflict pain upon ourselves, we are shunned as masochists.

Yet even this is not always true. People will praise us for certain kinds of suffering we bring upon ourselves. If we die for our country, or lay down our life for a friend, or are martyred in the fight for racial justice, we will likely be treated as some kind of hero and our actions held up as good and holy examples for others to imitate as best they may. Far from being necessarily evil in themselves some kinds of pain and grief are hailed as signs of goodness or even holiness.

God on Trial

We accept and even embrace an incredible amount of pain and grief so long as it has some meaning or purpose for us or for others. It seems evil only when there appears to be no point to it. Then the only way we can make sense of this kind of suffering is to blame someone. And if we cannot blame someone we know, we tend to pin the blame on a God we do not know.

Yet we do not blame God for every catastrophe or cosmic disruption. No one questions the power or the goodness of God because level fields suddenly erupt into massive volcanoes or earthquakes hurl mountains into the sea. We do not mourn the death of mountains nor blame God for the destruction of fertile fields; we doubt His goodness only when people are living on the side of the mountains or ploughing the fields when they erupt. So long as all the violent cataclysms of the universe form one harmonious whole, we can accept that God knows what He is doing and even marvel at the balance of nature demonstrated by these potentially catastrophic cataclysms. We question God's goodness only when human suffering follows in their wake.

Death and destruction in themselves do not make us doubt God's goodness, only the personal suffering that accompanies them. The problem of evil is really the problem of our own sensitivity and self-consciousness, so that when we ask about all the evil in the world we are really asking about our own feelings. We need to know why we feel so empty when our friends reject us and why something dies within us when our son dies of cancer. Why do we feel so distressed and even guilty when we see the distended bellies of starving African children, or feel disgust and anger at the massacre of three million Cambodians in the "Killing Fields"?

Before we can blame God for all these evils, we will have to blame Him for making you and me the kind of creatures who are able to suffer all this pain and grief. What does God find so precious about us that He will not give it up even though it brings much anguish to our lives and to the lives of others?

Most people think that it is a good and holy thing for us to get upset about starving children and devastated when our son dies of cancer. They intuit that something very precious about our personality and character would be lost forever if we were suddenly unable to feel any pain and grief. It is as though, in some sort of mysterious way, being able to suffer, far from being evil, gives us a share in the very goodness of God.

This is not to say that suffering is something good in itself. People who think this way have serious psychological problems and can be a real danger both to themselves and to others. And if God likes suffering, He must be a real threat to His own creation. No, if God is really good, He must first of all find all the world's suffering more offensive than any of us can possibly imagine, yet at the same time not be able to get rid of it—not even the torture of little children—without destroying something of His own goodness.

Divine Constraints

There are certain things God simply cannot do. He cannot make a square circle because the idea of a square circle is nonsense and there is no nonsense with God. Nor can He fill a jug with water and leave it empty at the same time. Though He may decide to turn water into wine, He cannot do it without getting rid of the water. There are actually some things God cannot do that I can do. He is too good to tell lies or torture little children, but I can do both because I am not necessarily all that good. Unlike me, God cannot do silly or devilish things and still be true to Himself. He cannot have His cake and eat it too. So, should it turn out that our pain and grief—far from originating in some mysterious injustice built into the heart of the universe—are instead a necessary result of God's goodness, we can begin to understand why God cannot rid the world of all its suffering and still remain true to Himself.

It is because our pain and grief reflect something of the goodness of God that people treat martyrs as saints and think it is a good and holy thing to suffer for the sake of others. Far from being necessarily evil in itself, our suffering allows us to become more like God.

Suffering Because We Care

Electrons do not cry out in anguish when they collide with other electrons, nor do stones mourn the loss of other stones as they watch them passing into the dust of the earth. Crocodiles never grieve the death of their victims when they shed their crocodile tears. But when I collide with my fellowmen we both suffer for it, and I grieve when my friends return to the dust of the earth. I want to weep with those who weep and mourn with those who mourn, and these very tears make me more than just a cog in the wheel of fortune or an insignificant bundle of energy in a meaningless universe.

If you were not aware of your own anguish and knew nothing of other people's tragedies, you would not know the evil of suffering, but you also would know nothing of caring for others nor ever share their loves and joys. Along with life and birth you would endure death and utter devastation, but you would be equally indifferent to both, feeling neither joy nor grief, neither gain nor loss.

If it were not for your ability to suffer, you would be nothing more than a plaything in some kind of divine playground, created simply to satisfy the whimsical pleasures of arbitrary gods indifferent to your own fate and to the fate of all the other playthings. To be unaffected by the tragedies that come your way would be the worst evil of all, for you would be devoid of all those personal feelings and affections that make up your unique personality.

You suffer pain and grief only because you care. You grieve the loss of your leg only because you care about walking; you mourn the loss of your friends only because you love them. This caring and suffering sets you apart from the dog who bites your leg or the cancer that riddles the bodies of your friends. God cares for you so much that He allows you to care along with Him. And because you care you also suffer.

Sacrificial Love

If this is true of you, it must in some sort of infinite way also be true of God. You suffer because you reflect in yourself something of a God who loves you; in some small way your own acts of love reflect His infinite love. It is a love which, like every kind of love, never follows the rules of logic. The heart does not have its reasons, contrary to what is sometimes said. Or rather it has no reasoning beyond itself. I have no idea why God loves you and gave you the power to reflect something of His love, just as I do not know why He happens to love me. Even my closest friends are quick to point out that I am not very lovable. Yet I know God loves me, just as He loves you, because if He did not, He would never have made us in the first place. And I am rather glad that He did, even with all the pain and grief that goes along with it.

If my pain and grief come from love, they cannot be evil in them-selves. In a mysterious sort of way they must be an essential part of love's goodness. And if God is infinite love, it would seem to follow that He must have an infinite capacity for pain and grief. At the very least He must suffer when anything goes wrong with His creation, just as I suf-fer when something goes wrong with anything I have done.

Yet God cannot suffer physically because He does not have a body, and His heart cannot actually break because He does not have a physi-cal heart. Nor can He suffer from some sort of personal loss because God cannot lose anything.

As God neither suffers from any selfishness within Himself nor from anything inflicted upon Him from outside, it might be better not to use the word "suffering" at all when talking about Him. A much bet-ter word would be "self-sacrifice." Only by learning the meaning of sac-rificial love will we come to terms with our own pain and grief and find the key for solving the problem of evil. We must find out what it means to say not only that God cares for us, but that God Himself is Love.

10

All You Need Is Love

If only the poor benighted lamb was able to understand the true significance of sacrificial love, he would surely rejoice at the honor we bestow upon him as we lead him to the slaughterhouse in preparation for our Sunday dinners. With the same knowledge even the unfeeling cabbage, as it is thrown into the stewing pot, might appreciate that it is fulfilling a fundamental law of exchange governing the entire universe. By such noble and sacrificial acts the woolly sheep and leafy cabbage are miraculously transformed into becoming a part of something as marvelous as us.

Life out of death

So it is at every level of life. As the insignificant minnow is sucked into the maw of the awesome whale, should it not rejoice that it has contributed to the whale's might? Were not the ancients right in killing the kingly lion not just for food but for its skin which, when worn in solemn ceremony, might bestow upon the killer something of the lion's strength? Is it too much to hope that in some unknown heavenly realm the potential chicken will be thankful that it has sustained us by never progressing beyond the docile egg we consume for breakfast, or that the very rocks and rotting vegetation that now lie lifeless on the autumn ground shall one day sing their silent praise to the god who made it possible for them—by their unstinting act of quiet sacrifice—to be transformed into the soil in which we plant the cabbages that give us life. It would seem that even in the autumn leaves there are signs of a universal law of sacrifice transforming everything into a future glory beyond our wildest dreams.

Just as cabbage heads and kingly lions are transformed into the glory of our humanity simply by being eaten, so by our own personal sacrifices we can be caught up into realms inhabited by the gods. Imagine the thrill of being chosen as one of your tribe's annual human sacrifices. Lying upon the burning pyre or standing above the yawning chasm waiting to be thrown to the expectant gods, you would know that you were the very best your tribe could offer, and that in some mysterious way you were making it possible for your family and all your friends to fulfill their own eternal destiny. For a moment, fear of the unknown might have held you back from the brink of certain death, but then all hesitation would have been overwhelmed by the same rush of exaltation and excitement a young man or woman might feel today if chosen to represent their country in the Olympic games.

A Fatal Flaw

There was, however, one small but serious flaw in all these ancient practices. Sacrificial offerings require sacrificial victims and the victims always end up the worse for wear. Unlike the Olympic games where participants usually have some hope of winning, sacrificial victims lying upon burning pyres or falling into yawning chasms always appear the losers. What is true of men and women is also true of sheep and cabbages and every other kind of sacrificial victim, so that even though you may become healthier by consuming your breakfast egg, you hardly do the potential chicken any good. It is difficult to see how there can be any justice in a law of universal sacrifice that gives us strength and glory only by victimizing creatures weaker than ourselves or create new life by preying upon the lives of others.

We can, of course, attempt to bypass this universal law of sacrifice or at least minimize some of its worst effects. We have now given up throwing people over cliffs or burning them alive on funeral pyres, and I suppose we could all reduce the massacre of unborn chickens and ease the hurt of slaughterhouse sheep by becoming vegetarians. But even then, if we are to save our own lives, we would still have to slaughter the insentient cabbage. Also, by refusing to sacrifice the lamb in the slaughterhouse of human gluttony, we do not save its life. Instead we only allow it to die a natural death where it ends up fertilizing the ground from which the insentient cabbage grows. Even for the vegetarian it seems there can be no life without some form of sacrificial death.

If you sacrifice yourself to either gods or men, your only sure reward is death, and by giving your life away you lose only what little life you have. Should you be re-incarnated after your untimely death into some other form of earthly life, as some people like to think, it still would do you little good, for what you might become would have no connection with what you once had been. By becoming something other than yourself, no matter what, you would lose the only life and personality, character, and humanity you ever had.

Keeping What You Give Away

You not only lose your life by giving it away, you cannot even give away your prize possessions and still keep them for yourself. When Suzie asks to have a bite of Joey's chocolate bar, he quite sensibly refuses to give her any if he wants it all for himself. Though we may scold him for being selfish, we certainly cannot condemn him for being stupid. Yet there are some things Joey can give away and still keep for himself, or may even end up having more as a result. If he is watching a television show and refuses to let Suzie into the room because he wants to watch all of the show, or will not tell Suzie about a story he is reading because he wants to know the entire story, we are not so likely to criticize him for being selfish as to laugh at him for being so incredibly foolish. He ought to realize that he will not know any less of the story by telling Suzie what he knows, nor will he lose any of the television program by sharing it with others.

Of course, real children are quite aware of this. If Joey tries to keep Suzie out of the television room, it is not because he wants to keep all the television show for himself, but because he is afraid that by talking all the time or by finding other ways to draw attention to herself, she may ruin the show for both of them.

Such childish bickering is an important clue to the secret of our own personality. Joey and Suzie teach us that although physical things like rocks and chocolate bars are lost by being shared, many other things—such as knowledge and pleasure and love—need to be shared in order to be fully enjoyed. Sharing what we know and the pleasures we enjoy actually clarifies our knowledge and intensifies our pleasures. Even though you cannot give away your chocolate bar and keep it for yourself, you will enjoy chocolate bars all the more when others enjoy them with you.

All good teachers know that the best way to learn is to teach. In similar fashion most of us enjoy a Rembrandt painting or Beethoven symphony much more when we are enjoying them with someone else. And when we are caught up in the enthusiasm of a large crowd of like-minded people, as at a rock concert or political rally, our minds can be dramatically transformed by the general mood of the crowd. As we are carried away by the crowd's enthusiasm, we discover feelings of love or hatred within our hearts we never knew we had. By losing our self-consciousness we find new life. By dying to ourselves we suddenly come alive.

Dying to Self

The greatest mystery in life is the undeniable fact that when we are not thinking about ourselves, we begin to find ourselves. If you get involved in helping old-age pensioners or in protecting the rights of little children, you contribute something towards their welfare, but if you start worrying that you may have nothing to contribute, you will spend most of your energy thinking about yourself and eventually give up helping others altogether. At a party you may get so caught up in the conversation that you completely forget about yourself, only to realize when you get home that you were really quite clever. But if you start wondering at the party if you are being clever, you will almost certainly end up a bore. In the same way a musician gives a good performance only when he is so absorbed in what he is doing that he does not have a chance to ask himself whether he is giving a good performance. He makes mistakes only when he starts thinking more about his ability to play the music than about the music he is playing.

Personal sacrifice in itself is not necessarily destructive. Certain things like knowledge and love and pleasure actually grow by being given away. And by dying to self you actually begin to live a fuller life. Perhaps this is why we are profoundly moved by films depicting soldiers sacrificing their lives to help their buddies escape from wartime prison camps, or why our hearts go out in wonder and admiration to the Polish priest Maximilian Kolbe who, in exchange for the life of one of his parishioners, offered himself up to a slow and tortuous death in a Nazi prison camp. When we see film clips of Martin Luther King Jr. crying out, "I have a dream" or watch Mother Theresa caring for the lifeless poor in the forgotten streets of Calcutta, we are stirred by an emotion greater than mere admiration.

We respond in awe to a love far different from the popular self-centered love which cries out to the beloved, "I desperately need you and cannot live without you." There is a sacrificial love as hard as life itself, a love that is willing to give everything to another without counting the cost and which we need to cultivate in ourselves if we are to survive this life with any real peace of mind.

Self Preservation

You may want to give your life away for the sake of others, and may at times wish you could be a hero of self-sacrifice like Martin Luther King, Mother Theresa, or Maximilian Kolbe. Yet fear holds you back, just as it once held back the human victims of ancient sacrificial rites. Though something within you wants to be a modern martyr, a much stronger force urges you to preserve the comfort and security of your life just as it is.

The instinct for self-preservation usually wins the day. Far from handing ourselves over to sacrificial love, we strengthen our defenses and raise protective walls whenever we feel threatened by love's demands. Knowing that life is fragile and that pain and grief inexorably follow in the wake of personal sacrifice, we avoid getting too involved in other people's lives and learn instead to stand on our own two feet. Desperately searching for security, we shrink back in fear at any suggestion that we might actually find our real life by losing it; we defend ourselves by arguing that God helps those who help themselves, or, in a less religious vein, that if we do not look out for number one, no one else will.

Such self-centeredness may not be very admirable but at least it makes good sense. The only trouble is that we are not nearly as sensible as we would like to think. Once we convince ourselves that we should look after our own self-interests and forget everyone else, the incomprehensible love of Maximilian Kolbe and Mother Theresa rise up to haunt us. Why is it that we can never rest easy with the logic of our own selfishness or be praised for being so sensible? Deep within us is a never-ending conflict between our own self-interest and the high expectations of sacrificial love such that either we feel guilty for being so selfish or foolish for being so loving.

Doing What Comes Naturally

No matter how logical selfishness may seem, none of us are as self-centered as we might like to think. We worry about ourselves only when there is something wrong with us. We talk about our feet only if we have sore feet and think about our heads only when we have a headache. We put ourselves first only when we feel under threat from others or from an environment indifferent to our basic needs. Most of the time we worry about family, friends, and colleagues, whether there is anything wrong with them or not; we think about children and animals and the place where we live, rather than about ourselves. And we are upset when they suffer, even though their suffering may be none of our business.

Sacrificial love just seems to come naturally to us. And no wonder. Such love has, after all, made us what we are. We would never have been born if there had not been some sort of love between our natural parents, even if it was nothing more than a pretense of "making love" at the time of our conception. And after our birth, an unending round of parental sacrifice kept us alive, and the sacrificial care of teachers at school kept us from turning into fools. Were it not for sacrificial love we would all be psychological wrecks.

Willing Victims

So far so good. You may easily agree that we need acts of sacrificial love to keep us sane, and that there is no real growth or even life without some kind of sacrifice. But this still does not ease the fate of those who are sacrificed. The slaughtered lamb and boiled cabbage may come into their own by keeping us alive, but they still remain victims of a never-ending struggle for survival that in the end they must always lose. Even the mother who sacrifices every personal pleasure to slave unceasingly for her children's welfare, as often as not ends up with little to show for all her efforts except disappointment and betrayal.

Yet there is all the difference in the world between self-sacrificing mothers and other sacrificial victims. Whereas others are led unwillingly and unknowingly to their untimely deaths, a mother's daily acts of personal sacrifice are done willingly in love. Not only that. Far from destroying her, these acts of sacrificial love give her strength and creative energy.

We grow spiritually and creatively, not by clinging to ourselves or to what few possessions we may happen to have, but by giving ourselves to others so habitually and completely that gradually a mysterious and explosive exchange of character, interests, and personality takes place in the deepest recesses of our united souls.

And what is true of us must be preeminently true of the God who made us. The explosive force or "big bang" which created our world must have come from an overwhelmingly powerful act of divine sacrificial love.

Love really does make the world go round, and self-abandonment is the key to creativity.

The Revolution That Failed

We have all been told that God is love, but few of us took much notice until the sixties generation came along. Then all of a sudden we were told that "all you need is love." The gospel of love was shouted from the housetops by longhaired hippies and screamed through amplifiers by rock musicians. A new faith taught the world that its problems would be resolved by love, and a new morality demanded that nations make love, not war.

It all seemed terribly exciting at first, but then a cynical generation turned its back on youthful optimism and wrote off love as the unrealistic morality of a hopelessly romantic idealism.

Yet the young prophets of the sixties did not fail because their message of love was unrealistic. They failed because they never became radical enough to fully grasp the meaning of their own message. The Hollywood films of the thirties and forties had made them—along with all the rest of us—far too sentimental to understand the real meaning of love and much too soft to put into action the love they proclaimed. Too idealistic ever to become true revolutionaries, reaction was bound to set in and aggression take the place of sentimentality. Punks succeeded hippies and substituted hate for love, knowing that life is neither a bed of roses nor a refuge for flower children. Instead of making love, they blew their minds with drugs until even the drugs betrayed them and their hearts drowned in a torrent of self-pity and remorse.

The slogans of love went sour because they failed to point out that love is a two-edged sword that, though it may make the world go round, all too often makes the world go wrong. As well as being the source of life, love is also the cause of almost all our pain and grief, teaching us the bitterness of tears even as it holds out the hope of personal fulfillment and happiness.

Unrequited Love

All of us need to love and be loved and, under the surface of our lives, there is a lurking fear that our need for love will remain unfulfilled and our own love unrequited. The spiritual cancers of unrequited love are never far away, no matter how deeply we may bury them in the inner recesses of our hearts. We need a few people at least who are willing to sacrifice themselves for our sakes without any conditions or strings attached. We cry out to be caught up in that world of sacrificial love where men and women willingly lay down their lives for their friends. We need to believe that we are worth dying for; we need to be worshiped and adored through physical acts of sacrificial love. We need someone to say to us, as the old Anglican Prayer Book so rightly had a man say to his new wife in the middle of the marriage service, "With my body I thee worship."

When that worship is withdrawn and love unrequited, we feel alienated and intolerably betrayed, and our original love all too easily slips into unremitting hate. We discover a terrible disorder at the heart of sacrificial love which breeds spiritual death as well as life, destruction as well as growth. Living in a world strewn with the bodies and souls of every kind of sacrificial victim from rejected parents to neglected children, we too easily think that every sacrifice is the potential enemy of creativity rather than its source, and every loss the denial of personal fulfillment.

In spite of all the fruitless pain suffered by sacrificial victims and the anguish brought upon us by our need for love, most all Christians, and the Jews who went before them, have believed we were placed on this earth to order the world according to God's law of sacrificial love, and that self-centeredness creates a disorder so vast it can transform the whole planet—and even the entire universe—from a Garden of Eden into a Vale of Tears. Selfishness, they insist, is sin, no matter how logical it may appear and, as St. Paul put it, "The wages of sin is death"— death not only for ourselves but for the entire universe.

Witnesses to Love

Christians have also believed that love unleashes a power which is able to transform every human sacrifice from an instrument of victimization to a source of personal fulfillment. Though victimization and death are always evil in themselves, the deaths of the martyrs are not a defeat but the very food of the church, and the sacrificial lives of Mother Theresa and Maximilian Kolbe are not an illusion but an intimation of future glory. For the believing Christian, the death of Jesus either occurred on a Friday that was infinitely good—the best Friday there has ever been—or else every personal sacrifice is a waste of human life and the Mother Theresas of this world are benign but deluded fools.

If Mother Theresa was a fool, you can safely hide in your own self-centeredness. But if she, along with Maximilian Kolbe and so many thousands of others, hold the key to our ultimate happiness and personal fulfillment, then we must walk the road of sacrificial love no matter where it leads. There is no middle ground and none of us can stand at the crossroads forever.

Walking the Road of Sacrificial Love

But before any of us can walk the road of sacrificial love with any confidence, we need some evidence that love actually wins the day over hatred and selfishness, and turns to victory the apparent defeat of all the martyrs. In order to believe that God is love, you and I need to see how His love overcomes the meaningless death of countless sacrificial victims and conquers the tyranny of all our pain and grief. You will have to watch this God actually suffer in flesh and blood along with drug addicts and alcoholics, starving Africans and dispossessed fugitives, the persecuted and the homeless—and then see Him rise above His own suffering.

Above all, you will have to test this doctrine of divine love by examining the way love works itself out in your own life. You will have to experience love active in your own flesh and blood, conquering every hate and destroying every council of despair, for only then, without sentimentality or pretense, will you be able to join the cry of the sixties generation and once again shout their message from all the rooftops of the world:

"All you need is love."

11

At the Name of Jesus

When a French Republican strikes his thumb with a hammer, he is not known to cry out in pain the name of "Napoleon Bonaparte," nor do the English use Winston Churchill's name in vain or the Australians swear by "Kylie Minogue." People may pray to a madonna, but not to the star of Evita. Even the cults of Elvis Presley and Marilyn Monroe have never gone so far as to assume that their names have the power to curse or bless. Yet this is precisely what everyone seems to assume about Jesus, so that even the most militant nonbeliever shouts out His name when disaster strikes.

The Power of His Name

What is in the power of Jesus' name that both Christian and non-Christian alike hold it in such awe and reverence?

For 2,000 years those who call themselves Christians have believed that this power comes from the Jewish God of sacrificial love who, at a particular moment of history, in an outpost of the ancient Roman empire, took on the humanity of a Jewish infant. Then, when He grew up, the local government authorities killed Him late one Friday morning, only for Him to come back to life the following Sunday.

That at least is the claim, a claim that is utterly unique among all the religions of the world. Other religions have had their holy men and inspired founders but throughout the entire course of human history, only Christians have claimed that their founder was also their divine creator and savior.

Others have treated certain powerful and influential human beings as if they were divine, but only because they thought there was a spark of the divine in everyone anyway. Even at those moments in their history when the Romans treated Caesar as some kind of a god, they never thought that out of some overwhelming love he had created Rome and all its citizens. They never thought of him as the Jewish God of sacrificial love.

Platonists never fell down in adoration before Plato nor, until influenced by the Christian West, did Buddhists send out missionaries to tell others about a divine Buddha. Mohammedans have never claimed that Mohammed was Allah in the flesh, and even to hint at such a thing would be the height of blasphemy. Yet this is what Christians have always said about Jesus.

If you want to find God in the flesh, you do not have to choose between Jesus and some other claimant to the title. Jesus of Nazareth is the only human being anyone has ever claimed to be the one and the same God who made you, along with the rest of the universe. No other religion or philosophy has ever even conceived such a wild and preposterous idea.

"What Manner of Man Is This?"

This claim about Jesus was made by the last people in the world to ever think that any human being could possibly be God. Unlike the pagans who imagined that their gods often walked about disguised as men and women, the Jews insisted that nothing on earth could ever represent God, disguised or not. Certainly no human being could ever be God, and to suggest such a thing was even more repugnant to the Jews than it would be to a modern Moslem. Unlike their Roman conquerors who thought that the whole world was more or less divine, the Jews, as we have seen, were convinced that God was completely unworldly. If anyone on earth went around acting as though he was God Almighty, instead of laughing him out of court as we might do today, they would have had him dragged into court and condemned to a traitor's death.

Jesus Himself was put to death precisely because He talked and acted as though He was God Almighty. Unlike the neighboring pagans who would have simply added Jesus to their list of gods and then carried on with life as though nothing had happened, the Jews had no idea what to make of Him. "What manner of man is this," they asked, "that even the wind and the waves obey him?" And again, "We have never seen the likes of this before in all Israel, that the lame walk and the blind see."

Looking for a Savior

The Jews were not gullible people. Unlike so many people today and the pagans of an earlier age, they did not demand a miracle every time something went wrong in their lives. Nor did they expect divine thunderbolts to come suddenly crashing down upon the heads of their enemies, as much as they sometimes wished they might. You would never have caught the Jew with a rabbit's foot in his pocket or a horoscope on his bedside table. Even a king as powerful as King Saul was in serious trouble when he called up a witch from the dead in order to have his fortune told. Whereas the ancient pagan saw himself caught up in the unpredictable events of an unscientific world, the Jew looked for order in the midst of the world's chaos and saw the presence of God more in ordinary everyday events than in the miraculous and spectacular. The Jews were anything but superstitious.

Yet even though the Jews did not expect God to step into world affairs every time they turned around, they did expect Him to send someone who would deliver them from the oppression of the pagan Romans. He had, after all, sent Moses to deliver them from Egyptian tyranny, and after that, in the days of David and Solomon, He had made them a powerful and independent kingdom. Now, precisely because God is consistent in what He does, it seemed to make sense for Him to restore this Jewish kingdom to its former glory. By the time Jesus arrived on the scene the Jews were expecting a descendant of King David to save them from the Romans, just as Moses had saved them from an earlier oppressor. What never crossed their minds was that this savior, whom they called the "Messiah"—or, in the Greek language, the "Christ"—would turn out to be God Himself come to earth to save them from the tyranny of their own selfishness.

Tales of the Unexpected

On that famous Palm Sunday before the Jewish Passover feast, when Jesus made His triumphal procession into the Jewish capital, the crowds really thought He might be the Messiah they were waiting for.

He was, as the gospel accounts make clear, a direct descendant of King David and the "pretender" to the Jewish throne. If He had just given the signal, the people would likely have risen up against the hated Romans, driven them out of Palestine, and proclaimed Jesus, the son of David, their rightful King. What no one expected or wanted was that He would instead rise up against their greatest national shrine—the temple itself, harangue its leaders as though He was God Almighty, and then return to the country to have a quiet dinner with some of His closest friends.

This whole story of Jesus' triumphal march into Jerusalem reads rather like a tale of the unexpected. But this is typical of Jesus. He is always doing the unexpected and then treating it as perfectly normal. When He is only twelve years old, He acts surprised that His parents did not know that He had to spend His time in the temple going about His Father's business. In Cana of Galilee He acts as though everyone at the wedding feast should have expected Him to turn water into wine. And He seems taken by surprise that people are so amazed at His healing miracles. It soon becomes clear that Jesus wants everyone to expect Him to do the unexpected, and that by taking people by surprise He forces them to ask what kind of person He really is. "Where does this man come from?" they ask. "Whose son is He? Is He just one of the village lads, the local carpenter's son, or does He come from God?" The Jewish leaders think they have the answer. They insist that, whereas no one will know where the real messiah comes from, they know where Jesus comes from and who His father is. But to this Jesus declares that they have no idea who His real Father is, and that, if they did, they would believe in Him.

Jesus keeps pressing the point: "What do you think of the Christ; whose son is he?" And again, "Who do men say that I am?" Given the surprising things He says and does, eventually those closest to Him stop trying to find some earthly answer to His persistent questions and look for an unearthly one instead. Then, at long last, Peter comes up with the answer Jesus wants: "You are the Christ," he says, "the son of the living God." And finally, almost at the end of the story, Thomas, the skeptic, falls down at the feet of the risen Jesus and exclaims, "My Lord and my God!"

Jesus or Caesar

It is almost impossible for us to imagine how difficult it was for these first followers to decide that Jesus actually was God, the embodiment of all that is real and true. Having been raised as orthodox Jews, they knew that there could only be one God, and that if Jesus was God, He and the Father had to be one and the same God in much the same sort of way that you and your children belong to the same family. To be the son or the daughter of a Smith is to be a Smith, everyone in the family equally a Smith, no one before or after another. This is how these first Christians gradually came to understand Jesus. He was "God from God, Light from Light, true God from true God." Though as a human being He was not as great as God the Father, as Son of God he was His Father's equal.

Because most of the Jews could not accept Jesus as their Lord and God, they ended up choosing the tyranny of Rome instead. During Jesus' trial, when the moment of truth came, they renounced their ancient inheritance and national independence, crying out in a single voice, "We have no king but Caesar."

Every generation has to decide who they think Jesus really is. It is as important for you and me today as it was for the ancient Jews. Their answer affected all the rest of their history as a nation. Our answer will affect our whole outlook on life and everything we do from now on. If in Jesus, God has become a human being, then far from being just some ancient miscarriage of justice, the crucifixion becomes the sacrificial love of God worked out in human flesh. In the dark light of the cross, your life and mine suddenly take on a new significance and our suffering is radically transformed into a potential power for good. Accepting the crucified Jesus as God in the flesh makes suffering worthwhile and our lives infinitely valuable.

Who Then Was Jesus?

But how can you possibly know for certain that Jesus really is God? What evidence can I give you? That there was once someone called Jesus who lived in a small country on the eastern shore of the Mediterranean some 2,000 years ago now seems as certain as that Caesar lived in ancient Rome or Napoleon in Paris. Even though we cannot compare his writings with those of Caesar—because He never wrote anything,

nor venerate His tomb as we can venerate the tomb of Napoleon—
because He no longer has a tomb, we can get a clear impression of what
He was like from the writings of His contemporaries. From them we
learn that the wisdom of His teaching and His seemingly miraculous
activities attracted a great following among the ordinary people until,
while still in the prime of life, the Jewish leaders handed Him over to the
Roman authorities to be executed.

This much both Christian and non-Christian generally accept, and
it would be extremely foolhardy not to. Yet this does not answer the
question as to who this Jesus really was. Was He simply a great charismatic teacher or was He God Almighty? And what about the stories of
His miraculous birth, His walking on water, and His raising people
from the dead? Above all, did He actually come back to life after His
public execution, as most of His followers have always insisted?

You may find it almost impossible to accept these extraordinary
claims. Yet Jesus must have acted in some kind of extraordinary way, or
else why would He be remembered at all. He certainly is not remembered as a great intellectual or military leader nor even as an outstand-
ing philanthropist, and yet He left an impression on His
contemporaries that has captured the human imagination ever since and
given such power to His name that 2,000 years later people continue to
use it either to bless or to curse.

12

God in the Flesh

Most of us have neither the time nor the inclination to search out all the historical evidence we need to understand why Jesus made such an impression on the people of His day. You can, however, get some firsthand evidence of what He was like simply by reading the early records about Him in the books of the New Testament.

Some people are put off reading these books because they think they will be too complicated for them to understand and the language too old-fashioned to speak to their needs. But the books are not really all that complicated. It is just that we bring to them a collection of complicated and even contradictory images of Jesus that we picked up over the years from parents and friends and Sunday school teachers. There is Jesus meek and mild, but also Jesus the rebel kicking the moneychangers out of the temple. Then we have Jesus the simple storyteller, a sort of Hans Christian Anderson of His day, who for some quite unaccountable reason gets Himself into trouble with the authorities and is executed for treason. Then there is Jesus the benevolent wonder worker who spends all His time wandering about doing good for others—the sort of person we can all admire and perhaps even try to copy at times, but hardly anyone we would think of as a close friend or invite to one of our dinner parties.

This is the trouble with so many of our images of Jesus. Instead of being a real flesh-and-blood person like us, He is only a vague ideal, and a religious ideal at that. And none of this fits with the New Testament evidence.

Starting Afresh

If you are ever going to find out what Jesus was really like, you will have to rid your mind of all these images and start afresh. Try the experiment of picking up a book of the Bible as though you had never heard of it before and knew absolutely nothing of what it was all about. Pretend you have gone into your local library and discovered some strange and esoteric book called "Good News" by an unknown author simply going by the name of Mark. Curiosity gets the better of you. You check out this new discovery, take it home, and read it all in one sitting. When you finish, you realize that you have read a very different kind of book from any you have ever read before. Strangely, there is no physical description of the book's hero or any account of his family background. There is not even any reference to his childhood or description of his special interests, skills, or hobbies. How he made enough money to support himself and his followers is never revealed. Instead, you are given a picture of someone bursting in upon the scene of ancient Israel, driving out demons, healing the sick, and embellishing this highly dramatic activity with stories about God's compassion for the poor and His stern judgments upon the nation's leaders. Here is not so much a detailed biography of an historical noteworthy as an impressionistic portrait of someone whose personality obviously had a very deep effect upon the author.

This is at least true of the first half of the book. But in the second half everything suddenly changes. Without explanation the author moves from a general impression of this man's activities to a detailed eyewitness account of his last week on earth. And then, in the last chapter, there is a brief and somewhat sketchy account of how this man supposedly came back to life, almost as though the author assumes that the reader already knows about his rising from the dead.

The Ring of Authenticity

There is in this book a ring of authenticity. The portrait of the main character is painted in a disarmingly unselfconscious style, with no attempt to persuade nor any apparent concern for accurate detail. It is written with an irrepressible exuberance, almost as though the author himself is surprised by what he is saying. If you read other New Testament writings about Jesus, you find this same exuberance. A remarkable variety of authors present similar events and sayings in different ways and in different contexts as though they had a treasury of common memories that they put to paper as quickly as possible without any structure or preconceived plan. Events and sayings are told with a kind of machine-gun rapidity as little vignettes simply laid before the reader without explanation or embellishment.

Why should all these authors bother to make up such a story, especially when so much of it is remarkably hard to accept? And what about all those contemporaries of Jesus who would have known if the events described in these books had been made out of whole cloth? When there were so many people wanting to stamp out the early Christian Movement, surely some of them would have pointed out that the whole story was a pack of lies. Yet nobody ever did. Apparently everyone knew better than that.

Even if we allow that some of the details may be the embellishments of enthusiastic imaginations, we still have to ask what kind of man could inspire people to create such unlikely embellishments. What was it about Jesus that made His followers put into His mouth such phrases as "The Father and I are one," or "He who has seen me has seen the Father"?

One thing is certain. No one is ever going to put phrases like that into my mouth. And should I start talking that way, my closest friends would certainly do their best to keep it quiet, knowing that if word went around I might easily be locked up in a psychiatric ward as a menace to society and a danger to myself. Occasionally I have come across people who have acted as though they thought they were God Almighty, and I have even met someone who claimed that he actually was God in the flesh. But, far from having a great following of people trying to convert the world to his cause, he was isolated in a padded hospital cell reserved for the criminally insane.

Neither a Fool Nor a Criminal

With Jesus the situation is very different. Just about everyone agrees that He was neither a fool nor a criminal, and should you or I think He was one or the other, we would be passing judgment on ourselves rather than Him, for we would be calling evil what everyone else calls good and insane what everyone else calls sane.

A strange thing has happened. Perhaps without realizing it, we have moved away from the common idea that Jesus was simply a very good man or an extremely wise teacher. That was the last thing He could possibly be. Anyone who goes around appearing to bring people's friends and children back to life, and then telling them that they should listen to him as though he was God Almighty, can hardly be considered either wise or good. People who try that sort of thing are either very bad or completely mad, and those who try to encourage their cause ought to be exposed as dangerous frauds.

Throughout the last 2,000 years people have been trying to do just that. Powerful governments have attempted to wipe out everyone who has believed in Jesus, and in a quieter but more insidious way scholars have done their best to explain away all the stories about Him. Yet they continue to be told, and the followers of Jesus continue to grow. Governments fall and scholars keep changing their minds, but the beliefs of His followers stand more firmly than ever and the Christian movement grows more rapidly today than at any time in the last two millennia. Perhaps the New Testament writings really are fundamentally accurate portrayals of Jesus as He really was.

Who Then Was Jesus?

Who then was He? According to the gospel portrait He was an ordinary man very much like you and me but with extraordinary powers for doing good. He healed the sick and drove out demons, and He spoke with a wit and wisdom far surpassing the leading intellectuals of his day. Yet, as the direct descendant of King David and the rightful heir to the Jewish throne, He also claimed to be ushering in a new kingdom far surpassing anything ever seen in David's time or any time since. His was to be a kingdom of God's reign on earth, a kingdom which was to come in all its power and glory once all the peoples and nations of the earth believed in Him instead of in the ancient gods.

As well as claiming to be a new king of a new kingdom, Jesus also kept doing things the Jews of His day believed only God had a right to do. He healed people on the Sabbath day and told them that their sins were forgiven. He walked on water and calmed storms on the Sea of Galilee, just as though He was the same God of the storm who had once led His people from Egyptian tyranny through the waters of the Red Sea. It was even said that He had raised people from the dead. All this was too much for the Jewish authorities who condemned Him for acting as though He was God Almighty by crying out, "We have heard the blasphemy." For the political security of the nation, He was then executed on a Roman cross as a traitor to their religious traditions.

The Missing Body

Hardly anyone has ever doubted that Jesus died on the cross that dark Friday afternoon outside the capital city of Judea. The Jewish authorities even had a guard placed at His tomb so that His followers would not steal His body away and claim that somehow or other He had been raised from the dead. Yet the body has never been found and no one has ever venerated the tomb as His final resting place. Throughout the centuries people have tried to explain this away, and even now, almost twenty centuries later, someone has come up with the idea that instead of dying He actually fled to India where He lived to a ripe old age. But if you can believe something as unlikely as that, you might as well believe what the Bible claims to have actually happened: that He died and was buried and rose again on the third day.

Salvation Without Jesus?

Here, it seems to me, are the actual facts of the case. If you do not accept them, what alternatives do you have? You are not likely to add your name to that dying breed of atheists who have all but disappeared, and you probably have little inclination to make up a new religion of your own. About the only other alternative is to join the ranks of all those secular pagans who subject themselves to the arbitrary whims of the gods of our postmodern world: wealth or prestige, power, security or sex. And when these gods betray you—just as surely as they betrayed your pre-Christian ancestors—you may turn your back on them and perhaps join an alternative lifestyle community as a slightly old-fashioned hippie or modern revolutionary. Trying to find some kind of personal salvation, you may even dabble in the occult for awhile, or adopt the spiritual nihilism of Eastern mysticism and the esoteric techniques of transcendental meditation. Then again you may simply experiment with alternative medicine or with the latest DIY fitness fad of the West.

Or you may decide to follow the way of Jesus.

Victory Over the Cross

In the cross you may be able to see the sacrificial love of God being worked out in the language of earthly flesh and human sin. In the cross you may see suffering and death sharing in the explosive energy of divine love. Here you may discover why, for so many, the cross is the symbol of life instead of a cruel instrument of execution, a decoration to be worn as a medallion round the neck, and a sign of victory to be lifted high in the streets of our cities and over the altars of our churches. In the cross you may see how victory really can come out of suffering, and new life rise out of death.

Yet the cross by itself can give no assurance of love any more than death automatically leads to life. Other peoples have dreamt their dreams of life after death, and the world is strewn with the dead bodies of those who have given themselves to others out of loyalty and love. Yet only in Jesus do the dreams become real and the bodies return to life, for it was not the cross itself that brought new hope to the world but Jesus' victory over the cross.

To believe in the triumph of sacrificial love, you and I must actually be able to see new life coming out of death and new joy out of suffering. Otherwise, the cross illustrates nothing more than the sadistic nature of the human race, to be used perhaps by religious fanatics as a tree of bondage upon which they can nail all our spiritual anguish and our deepest sympathies.

Only when the followers of Jesus saw that He was able to rise above death were they able to cry out with Him, "Oh grave, where is your victory? Oh death, where is your sting?" (1 Corinthians 15:55).

13

Jesus' Uprising

Contemporary witnesses insist that they did not just see a ghost that first Easter morning and the weeks following, but a living man who could eat and drink and still had the wounds of the crucifixion in His hands and feet. Yet He was not the same as before. For one thing, He would appear unexpectedly in the middle of a room, say or do something, and then just as unexpectedly disappear again. It was as though neither His body nor His physical environment confined or limited Him in any way.

The Mystery Man

One of the odd things about this "new man" was that his closest friends often failed to recognize Him when He first appeared. In the garden where He had been buried, Mary Magdalene thought that the person she was talking to that early Sunday morning was the gardener. She realized only that it was Jesus when He called her by name, as He had undoubtedly done many times in the past. Something similar happened later that same day when two of His followers were walking to the small town of Emmaus, a few miles outside Jerusalem. They were joined by Jesus on the road but did not realize who it was until they arrived home together. There Jesus blessed and broke the bread at the beginning of their evening meal, and in that breaking of bread they suddenly recognized Him. They had been talking to Jesus all along and did not know it. But then, when the truth finally dawned on them, He disappeared. The same thing happened a few days later when some of His former disciples went fishing. They looked up from their work to see a mysterious stranger sitting on the shore. Only after they went to the shore themselves and the stranger fed them some of His own fish, did they realize that here again was Jesus. It seems as though His friends never knew for sure when some stranger might turn out to be Him.

Though His physical appearance seems to signal His personal presence, only those who are close to Him personally are able to recognize Him, or those who share a common meal of fish or bread with Him, or when they are all assembled together as His church. Apparently this new man could be with His followers in a variety of physical forms through which they could gradually come to recognize Him. A common meal and the community of His faithful followers, as well as a physical body, were all outward and visible signs of His inward and personal presence.

Whose Body?

Jesus had prepared His immediate followers for something like this the night before He died. Blessing bread and wine at their last evening meal together, He told them that this was His body and His blood, and then added that in the future they should also bless bread and wine as He had done, to make Him present with them again. "Do this," he said, "for the recalling of me." Here was a new way in which He would be physically with them until the end of time. But it was not the only way. After His resurrection He took the physical form of other human beings such as that of a gardener or of a stranger on the road to Emmaus. Later His followers discovered that He was personally present in each of them as well, and that—to the extent they were all filled with His Holy Spirit—they could recognize Him in one another. Soon St. Paul was talking about the church itself as Jesus' body, and Jesus Himself is reported to have said that what they did to the least of His brothers they did to Him.

And What About Us?

Yet even if we accept that Jesus became some new kind of human being after His resurrection, how can that possibly make any difference to us? There is a world of difference between believing that a long time ago one particular man happened to come back to life after he died, and discovering that your dearest friend who recently died of cancer has come back to life. If we found our friends regularly rising from the dead, the creative energy of God's sacrificial love would be fairly evident, but the claim that once upon a time a single person rose from the dead is no evidence at all. Even if Jesus really did rise from the dead, the fact seems so out of keeping with all the rest of our experience as to be quite irrelevant.

That would be true if the resurrection of Jesus was a one-time event, and that was the end of the matter. But suppose the resurrection of Jesus was but the beginning of a worldwide transformation for all time. Suppose the resurrection of Jesus initiated a change in the whole ecological balance of creation so great that from then on it deeply affected not only your life and mine, nor just the society in which we live, but the whole natural world as well. If so, then here was not simply an isolated miraculous event of long ago, but a radical new stage in a revolutionary process of transformation that actually began with the birth of the first human being.

When we evolved from lower forms of animal life and then domesticated some of the very animals from which we evolved, we turned life on our planet upside down and perhaps changed the future development of the entire universe. Now Jesus completes this transformation. "Behold," he says, "I make all things new." His resurrection ushers in a new era of earthly life in which not only His fellow human beings, but all created things have the possibility of living a new kind of life in a new environment. For the first time everything is free to be completely true to itself, stripped of all those limitations hindering its full development. Here is nothing short of a new creation or re-creation which Jesus inaugurates by His own resurrection. From then on a "new heaven and a new earth" is in the making, and Jesus becomes "the first fruits of them that sleep."

The Power of the Spirit

Christians believe that such a transformation is actually taking place through the power of the Holy Spirit whom Jesus gave to His church after His resurrection. Once His followers became used to the idea that Jesus might suddenly appear at any time, He told them He would no longer be with them in His physical body as He had in the past. Now they themselves were to be His resurrected body continuing His work on earth, doing even greater works than He had done.

It is through this same Holy Spirit that we continue to take part in the new resurrected life of Jesus and become His new earthly body. This is the Christian hope and the anchor of our souls. All of us are born with dreams of future glory we never achieve, and a craving for an eternal life we know will be destroyed by death. Our bodies simply cannot support our wildest dreams. Instead, they gradually drag us down to the grave and kill all hope of immortality. After Jesus rose from the dead, however, death itself is transformed into the gate of life. In our deaths we now share in His death, and passing through His crucifixion we rise with Him in glory. By his resurrection our deaths become the means of our perfection and fulfillment, our dreams of glory mere intimations of our own future resurrection. Death is revealed as the final step in our pilgrimage from earthbound limitations to a glorified freedom.

Death completes a process of transformation that begins with the death of self-will and self-centeredness. As we die to ourselves we are filled with the supernatural energy of sacrificial love, and a life of limitless power begins to work in us, gradually helping us realize that we are made for better things than a life limited by the confines of mere earthly power. We are able to develop new lungs for breathing a new kind of air, spiritual lungs which are able to breathe in that Holy Spirit Jesus promised to give His followers.

The Fear of Holiness

God initiates people into a new human environment where their ability to breathe in the Holy Spirit gradually develops to the point where they are able to live the resurrected life of Jesus Himself. The outward sign of this initiation is baptism, and in the breaking of bread, or Holy Communion, we actually take part in the resurrection of Jesus. We eat and drink His resurrected body and blood, so that they may infuse our own natural body and blood with the power of His resurrection. We gradually grow out of our earthly limitations through a process technically known as sanctification, which simply involves being true to one's self. By growing in holiness or sanctity, we develop the spiritual organisms for living in the supernatural environment for which we were originally made.

Growth in sanctity, however, can be a very frightening experience. We feel on dangerous ground, alone without support, wandering around without direction. Almost from habit we try to breathe in the Holy Spirit with our old natural hearts and minds, originally designed only for earthly everyday life. And then, when this does not work, we become frightened or discouraged and scuttle back to the old familiar environment, to old habits and former prejudices, where we feel safe and secure. Like the ancient Jews, led out of the confines of Egypt by Moses, we cry out, "Why have you led us into this wilderness to die?"

So it has always been, this scuttling back and forth, even before the dawn of the human race. I suspect that those prehistoric amphibians who crawled out onto the dry land for the first time, would, if it were possible, also have cried out in fear, "Who has led us from the comfort of the sea to die in this arid wilderness?"

14

Cosmic Revolutions

When I was growing up, the natural sciences fascinated me more than any of my other studies. I devoured every book I could find on geology, astronomy, and basic physics. I used to sit for hours imagining dinosaurs crashing through prehistoric forests, while little horses—no bigger than a pet dog—played about my feet and giant dragonflies whirred above my head. In my mind's eye I could see that first stupendous moment when a solitary fish laboriously crawled out of his watery environment to breathe air for the first time. Inwardly I honored him for that daring act which eventually led to the birth of Michelangelo and Einstein, to space travel and, alas, the atomic bomb. Yet there was something I could never figure out about that gracious fish that took such a giant step on the evolutionary ladder of biological progress. Though I could appreciate his foolhardy audacity in climbing onto the beach in the first place, I could never figure out how he was able to survive once he got there. Wherever did he get the lungs that made it possible for him to breathe this new rarefied air?

The Comfort of Evolution

I still cannot figure it out, in spite of all I have since learned about the evolutionary process. According to Darwin's original theory, animals and plants very slowly and almost imperceptibly developed new organs and other physical characteristics by adapting to their local environment. Dogs learned to bark to scare off enemies and fish developed fins in order to swim. But why, I wondered, should a fish develop lungs to breathe an atmosphere he had not yet encountered and adapt himself to an environment that had nothing to do with his own watery world? It seemed obvious to me that when that first fish moved out of the water to breathe the air of dry land, the earth was not witnessing another stage in a slow evolutionary development but a radical and revolutionary change in its entire way of life.

The theory that everything—including the human race—slowly evolved from simpler forms of life without any sort of dramatic or traumatic upheaval was extremely reassuring to the people of Darwin's day. Following the upheavals of the French Revolution, the notion of change or progress through slow gradual evolution, involving almost imperceptible growth, rather than through political revolution or biological upheaval, appealed to people everywhere and especially to the English.

What the Victorians ignored, however, and what biologists have since recognized, is that there are sudden major jumps forward in biological development that raise life to new and unexpected levels. Some creatures are suddenly able to do things never dreamt of before, though in hindsight we can see that the original creature had the potential for some such development. Fish, for example, had always been able to breathe, but suddenly one of them started to breathe in such a totally new and unexpected way that we now feel compelled to call it an amphibian instead of a fish. For some mysterious reason a wayward fish seems to have already adapted itself to a way of life he had never known and to an environment he had never experienced.

I cannot explain the mystery, for though species may develop by adapting to their present environment, this does not help me understand how the first sea creature came to breathe air on dry land and become a new genus. All I know is that it could not just lie there on the beach waiting for its gills slowly but surely to turn into lungs, for, if it had, it would have been long dead before it ever took its first new breath. It had to have some kind of lungs before it needed them.

The Human Revolution

There are many sudden jumps like this in the evolutionary process that cannot be explained by gradual development. Among them is the unexpected appearance of men and women like you and me. Though animals have always known all sorts of things, now all of a sudden one of them knows that he knows. He can put sentences together and make decisions for himself. Whereas before there was an animal living by instinct, now there is a person living by his understanding. Until that moment there may have been creatures very much like this first human being, but they were not the same. The first human being may likewise have been a very undeveloped human being but it was human nonetheless.

The first book of the Bible is very clear about this, and what it says makes a great deal of sense. We have no purely scientific evidence, of course, that at a particular moment in our planet's history Adam and Eve suddenly appeared as its first human beings. We may, if we wish, believe that two other people appeared instead, whose names we do not know. Or perhaps several people suddenly appeared at the same moment in different parts of the world, though such an idea seems to stretch belief in coincidence almost to the breaking point. What we do know is that at a particular moment in time a new genus of animal—which for the first time could think reflectively and make free choices—suddenly appeared on the world scene where no such creature had been before. Call it mutation or divine creation or whatever you like, but the fact remains that human beings are qualitatively different from all that preceded them and are, so far, on the top rung of the evolutionary ladder.

The Next Rung of the Ladder

Ever since I can remember, people have been trying to guess what the next step on this ladder might be. The first theory I ever heard was that we would all eventually lose our little toes. Later, others who were perhaps a little more visionary suggested that our brains would get bigger and bigger as we adapted to the ever-increasing amount of information that keeps bombarding us day after day. Either theory may be true for all I know, but I must admit that even though the outside toes on my own feet are not very large, I have no reason to believe that they are any smaller than those of my grandfather or even of my prehistoric ancestors, and as for our brains, I sometimes wonder if they might actually be getting smaller. We certainly seem rather short on Platos and Michelangelos these days. The important question, however, is not how our race may gradually lose a few toes or grow bigger brains. What most of us want to know is what kind of superior creature, enjoying a completely new quality of life, may suddenly spring from our race just as we first sprang from the apes.

A New Creation

For the last 2,000 years Christians have been saying that this superior creature has already arrived on the scene. They claim that when Jesus crashed through the earthly limitations of human life by rising from the dead, a radical change in human development took place, so that even though there was an obvious continuity with the Jesus everyone had known before, a new man rose up out of the tomb capable of living a new kind of life. In the uprising of Jesus, a giant step in human development occurred which no one had expected and which for many people still seems beyond belief.

People find it easy enough to believe the Christian claim that after a false trial based on trumped-up charges, Jesus was executed for treason by the Roman authorities for supposedly claiming that He, rather than Caesar, was the true King of the Jews. They find it much more difficult to believe the further claim that early on the first day of the following week He was alive again.

The common skepticism about the resurrected Jesus is not dissimilar to what most of those ancient fish, still swimming about in the sea, must have felt about the first amphibian. The vast majority probably saw this new land creature as nothing more than a fish out of water, and believed that those who followed him were mere misfits trying to live above their station. Undoubtedly, many of them would have denied that land creatures could even exist.

Yet on that day when the first fish breathed a radically new kind of air, I can imagine the stars singing out in wild anticipation and the entire universe trembling in awe at a development that would some day give birth to you and me. Here was a fundamentally new creature, yet one which had developed from the old. Here was a creature which had begun its life as a fish and still retained characteristics of a fish, but which had been so transformed that it could rise above all the limitations of its watery environment.

Rising to Inaccessible Heights

In Jesus' resurrection we seem to be witnessing an even more dramatic mutation of earthly life. Suddenly, all that is personal gains complete control over its material environment, including the biological components of its own body. Jesus' body now becomes a perfect expression of His own personality. He was always fully human, and when He rose from the grave He was as human as ever. But now He enjoyed a new form of life capable of living in a heavenly environment. Before He was crucified He had the natural capacity to live somewhat above His bodily and earthly limitations, but after the resurrection He was able to do so completely.

This new "personalized body," or what the Bible calls a "spiritual body," is a much more radical stage in the evolutionary process than either the original transformation of chemical elements into life, or of fish into land animals, or even of mammals into reflective human beings. Yet no matter how radical this ultimate transformation may be, it is not inconsistent with what has gone before. From our perspective we may call it a move from the natural to the supernatural or from the personal to the supra personal, but seen from the perspective of the final goal of the whole evolutionary process, this latest transformation is the most natural of all, for it is the final fulfillment of all that life was capable of becoming in the first place.

Just as there was something about certain sea creatures that made it possible for them to develop lungs that could breathe the air of dry land, so there must be something about human beings like us that makes it possible for us to live a resurrected life. We only discovered we could live this kind of life, however, when Jesus actually rose from the dead, just as it was only after a sea creature found itself on dry land and started to breathe air for the first time that land animals could cover the earth. The resurrected Jesus shows us that our dreams of glory can come true, and that there is something about you and me that makes us able to live a greater life than we would ever have thought possible.

Yet we cannot do this by our own efforts nor live this kind of life by our own power. Someone other than ourselves must raise us up to inaccessible heights, just as Jesus—though He had the inherent capacity to rise from the dead—could do so only through the creative power of God. We can live a new kind of life, but we can no more create that new life for ourselves than bricks and mortar can turn themselves into a new house.

Living Beyond Our Means

There are many who have learned to live this new life and breathe this new air quite freely and easily, even if only for very short periods of time. They have had a foretaste of a life of personal freedom and of a power and energy beyond the possibilities of their own natural resources, making them able to endure the unendurable and achieve the impossible. Abandoning all attempts to save themselves, they have learned that when we let Jesus' resurrected life permeate our entire personality, we start to live a kind of life we could never have imagined before.

Christians believe that when Jesus rose from the dead, the mythical hope of all mankind became historic fact for the first time, and down the ages this same fact has continued to be multiplied in the resurrected lives of His followers. In rising from the grave, Jesus inaugurated a general uprising of the human race and set in motion a new revolutionary movement of the human spirit that is gradually transforming not only our humanity but the entire universe into the resurrected body and blood of our God. Here is a revolution in human history far greater than any revolution ever conceived by the most radical politician or social reformer, a revolution which no tyranny can suppress for long. This perpetual revolution shall be completed only when this era of earth's history comes to an end and there is a new heaven and a new earth, which shall themselves be the perfected body and blood of Christ risen from the shackles of our present death-ridden lives.

Part III

New Life

15

The Invisible Man

No one has ever seen God. That's why Jesus came to earth, so that by knowing Him you could get to know God without being able to see Him. At least that is what Christians have always claimed. But then, how are you to know Jesus? Where is He today? How can you find Him?

Jesus may have helped people learn more about God when He was walking the streets of Jerusalem, healing the sick and telling stories to His disciples. He may even have brought new life and power to His immediate followers after His resurrection. But that was a long time ago. Today there is no way you can sit down with Him for a long talk or run into Him on your way to work. He is nowhere to be found.

How, then, can I or anyone else expect you to believe in an invisible God by first asking you to put your faith in an invisible man? True, Jesus is said to have told His apostle Thomas that those people are blessed who have not seen Him and yet believe. But He also said that you can love God whom you have not seen, only if you love your brother whom you have seen. And as Jesus is supposed to be our brother, it would seem to follow that if we are ever to love an invisible God, we will have to find some way of seeing Jesus.

No Blind Faith

We believe, of course, in all sorts of things we never actually see. We have never seen the wind, but it would be foolhardy to disbelieve in hurricanes when we see knocked-down houses and overturned cars. Though we cannot see the wind, we believe in it because we see its dire effect on cars and houses. In the same way, a blind man will be aware of your presence once you touch him on the shoulder or call out his name. He will come to believe in you because of your effect on him. You and I are like blind men when it comes to Jesus. We cannot see Him, yet the faith of the Christian is not a blind faith. We believe in His living presence because of the things we actually do see and feel; things which we can only explain as the work of Jesus Himself.

But suppose you have never seen or felt anything to make you think that Jesus has touched you on the shoulder. You might still come to believe in Him if you could trust the evidence of others who believe they have been touched by Him, or trust those writers who insist that they saw Him in the flesh two millennia ago.

Though we may have little hope of ever going to China, we still believe there is such a place because we trust those who claim to have been there. I believe there was once someone called Napoleon because historians who have read his letters and other documents of the time tell me about him. Scholars may quibble over details of his life, but it would seem extremely foolish to conclude from their writings that there never was anyone called Napoleon. The same may be true of Jesus

Looking for the Invisible Man

What evidence then do we have for believing that Jesus, the Invisible Man, is alive and present with us today? What signs and witnesses can I offer to convince you that Jesus really is who Christians claim that He is, and that He is still at work in our world?

I can give you at least three. First, there is the Bible which Christians say reports the sayings and actions of Jesus when He was here on earth. Then there is the church which claims that in its teachings and rituals Jesus is still present with those believers who gather together in His name. And finally there is the witness and lifestyle of those who believe that Jesus has actually come into their lives.

That seems to be about it. If, after examining the Bible, the church, and the lives of ordinary Christians, you still cannot find good enough reasons for believing in the Invisible Man called Jesus, then there seems nothing for you to do but to abandon your spiritual quest altogether. Instead of wasting your energy pursuing a will-o'-the-wisp God you can never hope to see, you might as well hand over your life to the gods of power, ambition, and material pleasure that you *can* see. That is, after all, what many people have already done.

But before you follow their lead, let us take a look at the actual evidence, and see what hope there is of discovering that the Invisible Man is actually living among us.

If you are like most people, you are not likely to pin your hopes on coming to know Jesus either through reading the Bible or by going to church.

You will have heard just enough about biblical critics and certain scholarly bishops to believe that the Bible is quite incapable of proving anything. Certainly its writings are hardly the place they can expect to find hard evidence for the living power of Jesus Christ.

And magazines and television programs have probably given you the impression that the church is not quite sure what it believes or that it stands for anything of real consequence. Nor are the church's rituals likely to fare much better. Occasional attendance at baptisms, weddings, or funerals is hardly likely to inspire any sense of the living God.

For signs that Jesus is alive and well in today's world, you will probably have to begin with the people you know who go to church and consider themselves Christians. So let us first see if their lives can give you any reason for believing in the active power of the risen Christ.

Two Kinds of Christians

I don't know about you, but when I look at most Christians the first thing I notice is that their religious beliefs seem to have had almost no effect at all upon their character or lifestyle. Unless they are actually talking about religion or the church, they seem to be just like everyone else. Take away their claim to be Christians and nothing changes. There seems to be no real evidence that Jesus has touched their lives in any significant way. They may be pleasant or irritating, left or right wing in their politics, careless in their personal habits or overfastidious, but whatever they are, Jesus seems to have had little to do with it. It's true that most of them appear to be fairly good people, especially when judged by middle-class standards of respectability, but more than likely, that has less to do with them being Christian than with being middle class.

There are exceptions, of course. Some Christians talk about little else except Jesus Christ and what He is doing in their lives. But the trouble with so many of these people is that, on the whole, I do not like what Jesus appears to be doing. They seem so terribly earnest, always going about helping everyone but giving the impression that the less enjoyment they get out of it the better. They are good people, but appear to spend most of their time and energy attempting to make everyone else as good as they are, and criticizing all those who do not come up to their own standards.

I cannot imagine these earnest Christians hanging about, as Jesus is said to have done, with thieves and prostitutes and all kinds of disreputable people. They seem more worried about getting people to give up smoking than about society's outcasts. I don't think smoking is a very good thing, but I am not going to bother placing my faith in Someone who supposedly died and rose again simply to help us break the habit. Nor am I going to be interested in such a person if the chief purpose of His work is to bolster up current middle-class values. There are plenty of moralistic preachers, both inside and outside the church, who are quite capable of doing that, and they hardly need a resurrected Christ to help them along. If, of course, we can convince people to believe in a Jesus who wants everyone to be nice to one another, it will considerably reduce the work of the police. But the last thing I want is to be associated with a group of people who think of themselves as some kind of spiritual police force.

The Christians you like the most may very likely be those whose beliefs do not seem to have had much effect on their lives, and the ones who claim that their lives are based entirely on their beliefs may be people you do not really care for very much and certainly would not want to be like. It would seem, then, that either Jesus is not having any real effect on people or the effect He is having is not very good.

Clark Kent to Superman and Back Again

Is there any hope, then, of finding the transforming power of Jesus in any of your Christian friends and acquaintances? I think there is, in spite of so many appearances to the contrary.

We may have been too hard on our friends. Christians, after all are weak, frightened, and insecure human beings just like everyone else. They do not suddenly stop being themselves just because they become Christian. No one ever suggested that that would happen. Most Christians do not claim that they have been changed overnight, but only that they have been given a new hope and a new strength in spite of their weaknesses and fears. They have a new life but the same old character they had before, and like the first amphibians, they continually scuttle back and forth between the two.

That's not to say that there isn't any change. But the change is a gradual one that continues over a lifetime. It doesn't happen all at once. Transformation of character comes piecemeal, and most Christians are a strange mix of the life of Christ working in them and their old untransformed selves.

The practicing Christian is both Superman and Clark Kent. The latter we can easily understand for he is of the natural order of things, another ordinary human being like ourselves with all our weaknesses and failings. Superman, on the other hand, is a mythical figure representing our dreams of glory, a sign of our belief that somehow or other we were made for greater things than our ordinary natural powers make possible. In himself he is but a creature of our own imagination, but if from time to time we actually see Clark Kent turning into Superman, no matter how infrequently, then we know that a supernatural resurrection really must have happened and that we too are capable of living a life greater than our natural powers will allow.

Among the followers of Jesus we discover people already living this new kind of supernatural life. Not only are there people like Mother Theresa who have had a power for good beyond any natural explanation, but also thousands living in our own cities and towns whose sufferings make their simplest actions super-heroic acts of virtue. Then there are those who, while still on earth, have displayed various characteristics of Christ's resurrected body: Martin of Porres—who loved the sick and dying so much that he was seen looking after them all over the world, even though it is well attested that he never left his monastery in Peru—and others who were so united to the resurrected Christ that their bodies have defied the normal laws of gravity. Then there are those, such as Francis of Assisi and, in this last century, Padre Pio, who have had such great love for Jesus that they actually carried in their own bodies the wounds of His crucifixion.

Battle Scars

These are some of the super-heroes of the Christian faith, but they exist only on the horizon of our imaginations. For more accessible signs of the resurrection, you need look no farther than to your own Christian friends and neighbors.

You may have failed to see these signs before now because, as is true of most everyone else, you tend to like people who are like yourself. If you are not a Christian, you will like those Christians you only see when they have scuttled back into the habits of their old pre-Christian character. And some of the Christians you don't like may simply be living a life you have not yet learned to appreciate.

But like them or not, you cannot have any idea what sort of transformation has taken place in the lives of your Christian friends over the years. There is no way you can know what they once were nor what they would be like now if it weren't for their Christian faith.

There is nothing about an oak tree to suggest the insignificant acorn from which it grew. We can only compare the tree with greater and older oak trees nearby, and observe the damaged and broken branches that each tree has suffered as part of its continuous growth.

So it is with your Christian friends. There may be many things you do not like about them now, but you have no idea what they may have been like before you knew them, or what they may become in future years. You see only the battle scars and bruises they have received as part of their growth in Jesus Christ, and you are painfully aware of how much they still need to grow.

Punk Rocker

Whether or not we recognize the transforming power of Christ in people's lives depends upon what kind of transformation we are looking for. A young "punk rocker" from one of my former parishes, who was a recent convert to Christianity, was asked on a television program how he had changed since becoming a Christian. At first he replied that he didn't think he had changed at all, but then, on reflection, he added, "Yes I have; I am happier now."

This is the promise Jesus holds out for all of us. He died and rose again to make us happier, or more "blessed" as the older translations of Scripture used to call it. Our "punk rocker" was happier because he now had a future. He had hope, and this hope gave him new energy and a new confidence. He still had the same basic character as before and his own particular personality. That had not changed. But he now had a new purpose in life and was gradually discovering a new power within him that could overcome anything others might do to him. He no longer needed to defend himself because he was no longer afraid of being psychologically destroyed or personally humiliated. Instead of fighting other people, he could begin to love them sacrificially without counting the cost. If you met him today for the first time, you would find a pleasant young man with a lot of personality and charm and a deep matter-of-fact faith. Yet others who have known him over a long period of time realize that a change has taken place that cannot be explained away by his background, environment, or natural temperament. He has a faith anchored in a hope that more and more expresses itself in sacrificial love.

16

Signs of His Presence

Where does this faith come from? In our postmodern world there is virtually no encouragement to put our faith in anything or anyone. And what about hope? Despair and depression are more typical of the age we live in. As for sacrificial love, mutual self-gratification has taken its place as the guiding light in most personal relationships. Yet you probably know, as I certainly do, all sorts of people with an unshakable faith, with a hope that no catastrophe seems able to destroy, and with a genuine love for others that seems to override any thought of themselves. And I ask myself, "What possible justification can there be for such attitudes?"

As nice as these people may be, they don't seem to belong in today's world, and if they were sentimental fools we could write them off. But this just isn't so. Most of them tend to be no-nonsense sort of people, just as much aware of the facts of life as anyone else, if not more so. With all their ideals and enthusiasms they may at times seem to have their heads in the clouds, but they most certainly have their feet solidly on the ground. Their happiness is not due to some sort of whistling in the dark but to an inner energy and strength far different from what one would expect these days.

Where does this mysterious energy and strength come from? The ancient Jews believed that their own energy and strength came directly from God. In the same sort of way, these people, if they say anything at all about themselves, insist that their energy and strength comes from the resurrected Jesus working within them. And what other explanation can we give? In spite of all their weaknesses and failings, in many ways the lives of our Christian friends really are outward and visible signs of the resurrected Christ, and Jesus the Invisible Man really can be seen working within them.

What About the Church?

Though the lives of some individuals may seem to be outward signs of the Invisible Man, what about Christians as a whole? What about the church? Is it a collaborating sign of the risen Lord? On the surface it would hardly seem so. Far from helping people believe in the power of Jesus, all too often it is the church itself that keeps people from accepting the Christian faith. If the church is the power of Christ visible among us, the very Body of Christ as St. Paul calls it, what kind of body are you likely to see? Rather than the Body of Christ animated by the Holy Spirit, the church may appear more like a ragbag of weak, selfish, and desperate people animated by a spirit of aggressive self-centeredness who pretend to have something special which no one else really wants. You may be able to appreciate the idea that people who accept Jesus Christ as the living God should get together on a regular basis with their fellow believers. Yet this is a far cry from seeing how this body of believers can possibly give us any evidence that Jesus Christ really is the living God.

You look to the church for supernatural life and, likely as not, you find instead squabbles about minute points of doctrine and church leaders who seem more interested in publicizing their doubts than in building up any kind of faith. Instead of hope, all too often you find a general feeling of discouragement and discontent. And where you expect to find genuine outgoing love, you discover a closed and somewhat secretive society of people clinging to one another and ignoring everyone else—unless, of course, they can remake everyone else into spiritual clones of themselves.

Rather than finding a community living in the power of the risen Christ, all you may see is ineffectiveness and despair. Instead of that happiness or blessedness you may have found in a few individual Christians, in the church you are more likely to find a tense and earnest people eager to judge and criticize everyone different from themselves. Here, you may think, is no sign of the living Christ but the symptoms of a dying club kept alive only by the sheer weight of its own inertia, with no one left who has enough energy to kill it off.

The Body of Christ

How then can we still call this church the Body of Christ? I know of only one answer. The story is told of a devout Christian in the late Middle Ages who, after trying unsuccessfully for many years to convert a wealthy Jewish friend, learned to his dismay that this friend was taking a lengthy business trip to Rome. Surely, he thought, the corruption of the church in Rome would put him off Christianity forever. How great then was his amazement when his friend returned some months later, a committed baptized Christian. Asked if he had seen all the corruption in the church, the Jew explained that that is precisely what had converted him. It seemed to him that any church which could survive that amount of corruption for 1600 years must be divine.

This same church is still around 2,000 years after its Founder's ignominious execution. Its very existence is surely one of the greatest signs we can possibly have of the power of the resurrected Christ. If it were not for this, the church would have been dead and buried long ago. Instead, it is thriving and growing throughout the world in spite of continuous corruption within and attack from without.

Another surprising thing about the church is that most all the criticism we level against it comes from the teaching of the church itself. Church people may not live up to Christian standards, but it is only because of the continuous witness of the church that we have these standards to live up to. Though we may criticize the church for its lack of faith, hope, and love, it is only the church's teaching that made us realize the importance of these virtues in the first place. In a similar vein, we may criticize the church for not being a very forgiving community but at least it teaches the importance of forgiveness, whereas a non-Christian culture like Japan does not even have a word for forgiveness.

This is why Christians can be completely loyal to the church and yet constantly criticize it. The church is a self-correcting community, continuously being reformed and renewed by its own faith in spite of the sins of all its members, and loyalty to the church demands that we take part in its self-correction.

The weakness and immorality of the church's members give us some of the surest evidence for the active presence of Jesus Christ among us. The continuous spiritual power of the church and the high standards of its teaching could not possibly have come from its weak and fallible members but only from the living God.

The Biblical Evidence

Yet the life and teachings of the church and the sacrificial lives of individual Christians are not the only signs of the living presence of Jesus Christ. Christians also claim that reading the Bible should convince us of His presence. Yet this will depend on who reads. Highly educated people have just as frequently used the Bible to disprove the resurrection as to prove it, and as we see with the temptations of Christ, even the devil can quote Scripture. Many people have been taught to use the Bible as a collection of sayings they can haul out at any time to prove most anything they happen to like, whether it be genuine faith in God or their own private prejudices.

The Bible was never meant to be a collection of proof texts handed down by God as a verbal sledgehammer for us to knock down our opponents. Most of the Bible cannot be used to prove anything, but that is not what it was written for. Far from being a collection of proof texts, the Bible is a library of books chosen by the church to provide us with a record of one particular people's cultural history. The Jewish and Christian community compiled the Bible by selecting a variety of writings from its most representative authors, and these were then said to be inspired by God precisely because the culture they represented was itself inspired.

In the Bible you will read about the same weaknesses and sinfulness you find in the church. And like the church in every age, you will also read how God overrides this sinfulness and overcomes this weakness. In the Bible you will not read the story of good people made better by their own inherent strengths, but of bad people being made good by God. By reading the Bible to discern the action of God within the life of His chosen people, you will also discover all that God does for them. The common life presented in the Bible is very much the same kind of life you will find in the church today. Both church and Bible present us with the same continuous action of the living God, and you cannot separate one from the other.

Some years ago the University of Chicago published a collection of books called *Great Books of the Western World*, containing the representative writings of Western civilization in the fields of poetry and fiction, physics and philosophy, history, and art and just about everything else. Simply by reading these books someone from another culture could enter into the Western mind and learn what it is really like, and by absorbing the mentality of their authors could eventually become a Westerner. So it is with the Bible. By reading the various books within it, you and I can enter into the mind of the Jewish-Christian culture. We can become spiritual Jews and, according to Christian belief, in doing so we will also enter into the mind of God.

This can only happen, however, if you read each book in the spirit in which it was written. We do not read a mystery book as though it were a law book, nor should we read a Jewish myth as though it were history, nor an eyewitness account of the crucifixion as though it were myth. As with any other book you need to ask what the author was trying to say when he first wrote the way he did. Only then can you ask if what he wanted to say is true. If you read a mystery story in which the suspect's alibi depends upon him being in another town on Friday the 13th of June 1983, it makes no difference to the point of the story whether or not there ever was such a date. Should, however, the story be the account of an actual trial and it turns out that there was no such date, you had better ask for a retrial. In the same sort of way, you needn't worry about any factual errors you may find in the Bible, unless they actually affect what is being said.

If we find that in spite of factual errors, the different books of the Bible all present a continuous record of a people chosen by God for the salvation of the human race, and that one of their number, Jesus of Nazareth, fulfils all their hopes and desires and continues to do so for people today, then we have a clear witness to the truth of Jesus Christ and every reason to believe that God Himself was behind the writing of these mysterious books.

Walking the Road of Faith

Christians are sinful and foolish, the church is often corrupt, the Bible contains errors. Yet within all three are clear signs of the presence of the Invisible Man, Jesus Christ. There may also be signs of His presence within yourself. But the only way you will ever know for sure is by taking the first steps along the road of Christian faith and to start walking where millions have walked before.

$$\boxed{17}$$

The Return of the Gods

At this point you may be saying to yourself, "Walking the road of Christian faith may be very well for those who were brought up as Christians and know of no alternatives, but what about everyone else? There are, after all, lots of other religions in the world to choose from. What makes Christianity so special?"

True enough. I admit that I was raised in a Christian family, and given the society in which I lived there was little else I could have been if I was going to be anything at all. I grew up thinking that atheists and communists probably were not Christians, nor were murderers, thieves, or prostitutes, but everyone else certainly was, even if they did not do much about it. I still remember the shock I felt as a child when I first realized that my Jewish friends, who seemed just as good and devout as everyone else, were not really Christians. I had assumed that religion, goodness, and Christianity were all about the same thing, and that if someone suggested that so-and-so was not a real Christian, he was either prejudiced or vindictive.

Beliefs in Conflict

You may not have been brought up to think this way, but no matter how you and I were brought up, all of our thinking has been dominated by a pluralistic society of conflicting attitudes and beliefs. Some of these beliefs appear to be quite consistent with traditional Christian teaching, but others seem diametrically opposed to it. Most all of us were raised to believe that we should do unto others as we would like them to do unto us, but we were also told that God helps those who help themselves. Humility and a spirit of poverty were held up as virtues, and yet our parents often said that we should take more pride in ourselves and learn to stand on our own two feet. Anger was considered a sin, but it was all right if we called it righteous indignation. We were supposed to be nice to the little boy on the playground that no one could stand, and yet we were told that we were free to choose our friends. We were to practice discipline, but never repress our feelings; learn from others, but always express ourselves.

All these conflicting attitudes and beliefs have helped make us who we are. To deny any one of them would go against some vital part of our character and personality. Be we agnostic or atheist, Jew or Christian, we are all together in the same cultural boat where the religious labels we carry seem to make relatively little difference to our everyday lives.

All Those Other Religions

Just because so many Americans claim to be Christians does not necessarily make it right to be a Christian. Americans have been wrong about lots of things like segregation and Vietnam, and America has certainly had its fair share of violence and greed. Equating the American way of life with the Christian way of life does not really encourage us to believe that the Christian religion is much better or worse than any other religion.

In many ways the beliefs and attitudes of other cultures and other religions seem just as attractive as Christianity and the American Way of Life, if not more so. There is much to be admired in the American Indian's reverence for nature. Even the Hindu's sacred cows show a certain respect for the animal kingdom so badly lacking in our own society. The zeal of Islam and the family life of the Jews put the rest of us to shame, and the Buddhist has an inner peace we seldom see in our Christian friends.

You and I were accidentally born into a culture where Christianity was our most obvious religious option, but because it is obvious hardly makes it right. Nor would many people be so naive as to think that our Western culture is necessarily better than the ancient cultures in which Islam or Buddhism flourish. How, after all, can anyone these days possibly believe that by a providential accident of birth, some of us happened upon the one true faith, while everyone else got it wrong? Why should we think that the church down the road with its painfully boring services gives us a more certain road to salvation than a Buddhist temple? If asked to choose between different religions, even the most committed among us are likely to be somewhat hesitant.

Because the Christian lays claim to a unique revelation does not in itself make the Christian religion any better than those which claim only a profound spiritual insight. Christians alone believe that their founder was God incarnate. Fair enough. Yet there is no obvious reason why belief in an incarnate God should be better than other people's belief in reincarnated men and women.

And what are we to make of this claim to a unique revelation? What has actually been revealed that is so important? Whatever it is seems to depend upon what Christian you happen to be talking to. Different ones believe so many different things that it's anybody's guess which beliefs have been revealed by God and which have been made up to suit the whim of the believer. How are we to choose between Catholic and Protestant, modernist and fundamentalist, traditionalist and liberal? And if we do make a choice, how are we ever to know that the choice is right and that our final belief alone is true?

Perhaps all we can do is believe whatever we happen to like, and then own up to the fact that our beliefs are no better or worse than those of anyone else.

Agreeing to Disagree

We live in a world where television brings Buddhist temples and primitive religious rites directly into our living rooms, and where Irish Catholics and Protestants can kill each other with impunity before our very eyes. Thus it would seem that the best thing we can do is learn how to live and let live and agree to disagree, accepting the rather illogical theory that what may be true for you is not necessarily true for me or anyone else.

Though the theory may be illogical, at first glance there seems to be something quite wonderful about it. If, after all these centuries, we could give up insisting that we alone are right and that everyone else is wrong, bigotry might at last come to an end, and all of us could live together in peace and harmony. By some strange irony of history it may be that the peace we have been looking for all these centuries does not come from right beliefs, but from agreeing that no one's beliefs are necessarily right.

This sounds like great news, but it raises serious problems for committed Christians and everyone else with strong religious convictions. If the theory is right, then you can still believe in Jesus or Buddha or Mohammed, just so long as you do not believe in any of them all that much. Christians can still believe that Jesus is God, but only in the same sense that I can describe my wife as "simply divine." I call her divine because I love her, not because she is my Lord and Savior. The problem is that Christians have always believed that Jesus is their Lord and Savior and not just a special love object.

Why bother believing in Mohammed or Buddha or Christ and committing our lives to any of them, if we are not allowed to believe that our beliefs about them may actually be true? If all truth is relative and beliefs are formed more by cultural conditioning than by divine revelation, then the wisest course of action is to get on with life as best we can, and set aside the feeling that we have to be right as the relic of a more primitive and superstitious age.

Back to the Gods

Yet when we attempt to jettison this relic of primitive superstition, we end up right back in that primitive mentality from which we have so desperately tried to escape. Having encouraged you to walk with me on the long and difficult road towards Christian belief, it seems that we have now ended up in the quicksand of a dogmatic skepticism where nothing is right or wrong but only feeling makes it so. We have been thrown right back into that battle of the gods where the contradictory convictions of others and the pressures of everyday life threaten to tear us apart. It was precisely to escape this unending conflict and morass of uncertainty that I originally urged you to put your trust in the one God who is said to have revealed Himself to the likes of us.

Now it seems that we will only be able to live in peace with our fellow human beings if we abandon this quest for a sure faith and accept the fact that our efforts have been wasted and our desire for truth misguided. It appears as though we dare not believe in any particular divine revelation nor take Christianity or any other religion all that seriously. Instead, we are told that Christian and non-Christian alike must learn to accept one another with a strange new kind of charity that is willing to defend the convictions of those who deny our own and embrace the enemies of our beliefs as long lost friends in the faith.

When it comes to Christianity, however, this simply will not do. Christianity is a faith for skeptics but it is not a skeptical faith. The Christian claim is that we have been given an understanding of reality and human life that has come directly from God Himself. The Christian faith has not been discovered or invented, but revealed.

But how then can we possibly accept this divine revelation and, at the same time, not only live in peace with those who reject it, but actually respect and appreciate other people's beliefs radically different from our own? Is Christianity with its claim to a special revelation the source and perpetrator of every kind of prejudice and bigotry, and to be stamped out as soon as possible, or is there some important mitigating aspect of Christianity that we have not yet examined—something that will allow us to believe that we can be right without having to think that everyone else is wrong?

18

Beyond Belief

In order to hold fast to traditional Christian beliefs and yet live at peace with everyone who disagrees with us, we need to recover the ancient idea of heresy. Just like dogma, heresy has received such a bad press that most of us try never to think about it. Talk of heresy stirs up images of hate crimes, witch hunts, and idealistic reformers burning at the stake. Yet this is not what heresy is all about. Instead of stirring up hate, a true understanding of heresy is the key that makes it possible for us to appreciate everyone else's beliefs without forcing us to abandon our own. Contrary to popular opinion, heresies are not simply theological errors or beliefs that are utterly wrong, but beliefs that are not right enough. Heresies are not false beliefs but half-truths. Traditional Christianity has no word to describe wrong belief but only inadequate belief.

Far from being angry with anyone who calls you a heretic, you should run up and embrace him or her in love and thanksgiving for pointing out that the truth is far greater than what you can get into your small mind, and that there is always much more for you to learn. The very notion of heresy springs from the Christian virtue of hope, for it insists that faith is a continuous journey to be undertaken by the faithful and not just a present stance to be maintained.

All of us are virtual heretics and always will be. You and I are on a pilgrimage, continually probing the depths of the mystery of God. And others looking into those same depths, no matter what their formal beliefs or religious labels, will see facets of the truth still closed to me and make me realize how much there still is to learn. Far from threatening my own faith or discrediting the faith of anyone else, the intellectual humility which comes from recognizing our own heresies makes us face up to our limitations and forces us to appreciate the insights of others.

Beliefs Beyond the Pale

This does not mean that one belief is as good as another, or that we must accept whatever anyone says simply because they say it. We dare not go along with the religious beliefs that led a thousand people to drink from a vat of cyanide in Ghana at the end of the seventies or burn themselves to death in Uganda at the beginning of the new millennium. Nor can we respect the beliefs of satanists who practice and encourage child abuse. And, though I appreciate the religious beliefs of pacifists, I believe we must do whatever we can to stop people like Hitler and Saddam Hussein from massacring and torturing others at will. That broad-minded attempt to accept everyone else's beliefs, no matter how evil or contradictory these may be, can turn in upon itself and become the most dangerous heresy of all.

No matter how open-minded we might be, like it or not we are constantly judging other people's beliefs. We cannot avoid it, and if we try we will merely become allies of evil and friends of falsehood. We need some set of standards for judging the ever-increasing variety of contradictory and often bizarre beliefs offered in the marketplace of today's pluralistic society. Unfortunately, however, the standards we adopt are all too often based on little more than our own half-baked private opinions and limited insights. By grasping at straws of judgment, we all too easily end up nourishing our own most deep-seated prejudices.

Here again the half-truths that go by the name of heresy can come to our rescue. They remind us that falsehood does not come from being totally wrong but from being only partially right. We need to judge our beliefs and the beliefs of others by their comprehensiveness. There is a wholeness to reality that every belief must be able to accommodate. If a belief or creed or attitude is authentic, it will encourage us to believe still more and allow us to appreciate the insights enshrined in the beliefs of others.

Denying Denials

It is not what any of us actually believe that is wrong but what we deny by our beliefs. In judging other people's beliefs the only thing we need to negate are negations; the only thing we must deny are denials. I could never, for example, be an extreme puritan, for though the puritan is quite right when he insists upon the need for discipline, he is terribly wrong when he denies the goodness of earthly pleasures. Likewise, I cannot believe in reincarnation. The idea recognizes that human life must go through many forms of existence in order to reach perfection, but it denies the eternal value of my own unique personality by claiming that I am forever turning into something other than myself.

In the quest for wholeness and completeness, we will keep running into all sorts of popular ideas we cannot accept, no matter how attractive they may seem at times. I for one cannot believe that it is perfectly all right to get sexually involved with someone without marrying them. It seems to me that once two people start making love with each other, they dare not reject one another later on, and only marriage vows taken seriously make it possible for them to think that they never will. It's my very belief in the goodness of sexual love that makes me want to ensure that nothing destroys or damages it. In the same sort of way, my appreciation of femininity makes it impossible for me to go along with extreme forms of feminism. Because I believe in the goodness of women, I do not want to see anyone try to turn them into men.

Dangerous Heretics

Some attitudes and beliefs we have to condemn, not because they are totally wrong but because they parade themselves as being exclusively right. The trouble with the unrepentant heretic is that he shapes his beliefs to deny or ignore everything he does not fully comprehend and uses his limited knowledge to condemn the insights and understanding of everyone else. He takes the principles of socialism to condemn free enterprise or pursues the principles of free enterprise to further impoverish the poor. He uses the Bible to destroy the worship of the altar or the altar to ignore the spiritual demands of the Bible. In both church and society, he uses his inner feelings to rebel against all established authority or else upholds traditional authority to trample down every kind of innovation and renewal.

Heretics become dangerous when they refuse to accept that their thinking is heretical. Parading their limited views as the whole truth and their partial insights as the only true orthodoxy, they try to fit everyone else into the straitjacket of their own blinkered point of view. In so doing they become enemies of the fullness of faith and a threat to the peace and unity of mankind. Rather than trying to win others to their own beliefs by rational persuasion, these unrepentant heretics spend all their time and energy knocking down the conscientious convictions of those who disagree with them.

The Wholeness of the Faith

If you crave to grasp hold of all there is to know and desire to reach out to embrace the entire universe, begin by being skeptical of all your present insights and beliefs, recognizing that they are only partially right. Seek a faith that can remove the blinkers from your eyes and the prejudices of your heart. Desire wholeness, or what some call comprehensiveness and others catholicity.

You and I are made for greater things than our own limited experience can possibly provide. We have the capacity to know what far exceeds the preoccupations of philosophers or the speculations of theologians. We are more likely to find our vision of truth in the writings of poets and our picture of heaven in the works of artists. Yet even these can never satisfy completely. Our own imaginations, no matter how feeble, stretch far beyond the horizons of the Sistine Chapel or the innermost circles of Dante's Paradise. You and I have intimations of glory greater than anything that can ever be put into words or drawn from the artist's palette.

I started off by saying that I did not want to argue you or anyone else into Christian belief but only show that it is all right to believe. Now I have gone a step farther and made a plea for wholeness, a wholeness that comes only from a thoroughgoing skepticism that questions all our private insights, the assumptions of our culture, and the attitudes ingrained in us from childhood. Re-examine all your attitudes and beliefs. Do any of them enclose you in a mental or spiritual prison of limited insight instead of opening up a vision of reality greater than anything you could have thought of by yourself? Do they stifle your imagination or give you a deeper insight into all the intellectual and spiritual striving of mankind, an increased appreciation of every man's talent, and the achievements of every human civilization?

I believe that Christianity at its best can do just that. Christ has opened the door to the entire world of personal beliefs and human hopes. As Christians, we can believe what everyone else believes and yet believe so much more, knowing that our beliefs are but images of a larger truth, windows into a fuller life. Creeds and sacraments, holy books, and formal prayers are but glimpses into eternity, signs of a greater glory none of us can now see completely, but which will eventually end all argument and fulfil every human speculation. "Now," as St. Paul tells us, "we see through a glass darkly, but then face to face" (1 Corinthians 13:12).

Moving Beyond Belief

Belief in some sort of God comes from reasoned argument, but faith begins with dreams and ends in eternity. For now all we dare ask is that our dreams are vindicated by the undoubted action of God in our lives and in the lives of those around us. In exchange, all that God asks of us is that no matter what may befall us we continue reaching out to "taste and see that the Lord is good."

19

A New Beginning

This might seem to be the end of the story, but it is really only the beginning. So far I have tried to help you see that it is all right to believe. The next step is for you to find out if Christian beliefs are really right, and no amount of argument or demonstration can decide that for you. As I have already said, all you can do is walk the road of faith yourself and see where it leads.

Questions Along the Way

Your journey will begin with many questions still left unanswered, but this need not trouble you nor make you hesitate. The way forward in our understanding of God does not lie in having all our questions answered before we begin the journey, but by continuing to ask questions as long as the journey lasts.

The journey of faith is rather like those computer games in which, after every move, the player has to solve some new problem before he can move on. The answer to every question takes him a step farther along the way, but with every step some new question arises. So it goes to the end of the game when at last he finds the hidden treasure or goes into the royal castle or enters the kingdom of heaven. The questions and answers are all part of the game, and if you or I refuse to play until every question is answered and every argument proven we will never find the hidden treasure.

In the journey of faith some people act like stubborn children who refuse to walk until they are able to run or venture anything unknown until they are certain of their reward at the end. Too timid to take any risks, they keep wandering about in circles getting nowhere, demanding answers to every question that comes into their heads before they dare move towards anything of real value or importance.

Real flesh-and-blood children, of course, never act like this. They walk before they begin to run, and learn to walk by taking one step at a time. Everyone starts out on their spiritual journey like this as well, asking one question at a time. But then, when answers are slow in coming, some timid people give up asking and settle down at some wayside inn, the journey of faith unfinished and their inner desires unsatisfied. If you should be one of those, then you need to go back to your spiritual childhood and learn to ask all the important questions once again, pausing at every stage in your travels to digest what you have learned, but then moving on to ask new questions and discover new answers.

Traveling Companions

If you think that the Christian faith just might make some kind of sense, you need to test this faith by your own individual experience. Though Christianity is grounded in reason, only experience can ever convince you that it is actually true. Yet this is easier said than done. Our own experience is far too limited by our personal circumstances and individual temperament ever to be the final test of anything. We cannot travel the road of faith by ourselves and end up with anything really worthwhile. We must enter into the experiences of others who have traveled along this same road before us. Faith's journey must take place within the Christian community, for we can only see how faith actually works in practice by walking with those who already believe.

The journey begins with a baptism of water and the spirit which, ever since New Testament times, Christians have described as a kind of second birth. Originally the baptismal ceremonies and the experience of rebirth were so closely tied together that one was clearly a sign of the other. Through baptism a person became a member of a new community with its own unique cultural and social identity. He entered into a new set of personal relationships often more intense than those of his own natural family, and was given a new name, his "Christian name," which represented a new character and a new personality. In the very deepest sense he was "born again."

Those Early Christians

In the first centuries of the church's life, belonging to the Christian Church was an act of treason punishable by death; you had to think twice before getting tied up with this new outlawed community. It might be some inexplicable change in your closest friend, or perhaps in one of your slaves—something impossible to describe but irresistibly intriguing and attractive—that first arouses your interest. After pressing your friend or slave to explain this change they finally admit that they have become Christians. Eventually you decide to look into this new secret society yourself. They tell you something of the risks involved and the discipline required, but still you persist. Finally they take you to one of their secret gatherings in a large house on the other side of town. Here, to your surprise, you find several of your own personal acquaintances, your neighbor's two slaves, and several important town officials. The local plumber, who turns out to be the leader of the group and is called the overseer or bishop, quizzes you about your intentions, and then, finally convinced of your sincerity and integrity, he allows you to come to weekly meetings for instruction.

At these meetings, which are likely to last two or three years, the plumber-bishop explains all the Scriptures, beginning with the book of Genesis. During this time several of your fellow students are captured by the police and thrown to the lions, and you are made dramatically aware of the risk you yourself are taking. Still you persist, until the time comes when you are asked if you genuinely desire to become a member of this community of outlaws. You say that you do, the members of the local community vote to accept you as someone they can trust, and the day of your baptism draws near.

Initiation

On a Saturday afternoon you go to the bishop's house and renounce all the ways in which you are still tied to your past life. You renounce forever the gods of this world, the idolatry of your own appetites, and all the works of the devil. Exorcisms are said over you to drive away any evil spirits, and then you are told that you must not eat or drink anything until after you are baptized early the next morning. It is as though you must rid yourself of even the natural food that has sustained your previous life. This is to be a new beginning and a new birth, and nothing of the old must remain.

That evening, still having no idea what is going to happen, you gather with your fellow candidates and spend the night together in final instruction and prayer. Then, very early in the morning while it is still dark, you are led into another part of the house where there is a large pool of water. There you are stripped of all your clothes and made completely vulnerable, with no protective clothing and nothing you can hide from others. Nothing is left of your old life.

A healing and protective oil is poured over you as it was over the ancient athletes and, as the first rays of dawn come through the windows, you are taken by the hand down into the pool where you are immersed in water in the name of the Father who made you and all the world, of the Son who redeemed you and all mankind, and of the Holy Spirit who will make you holy along with all the faithful. You rise up from the other side of the pool and a white garment is placed over you, symbolizing a new life and membership in a new community. You are given a lighted candle representing Christ as the light of the world, and then, as a newborn member of the Christian family, you are fed with a spoonful of milk and honey, the baby formula of the day; you may be old in years, but you have again become a little child starting off on the journey of faith.

Holding your lighted candle, you and the other candidates are taken into the main hall of the house where all the members of the community are assembled. Amidst a sea of lighted candles you move to the front of the room where the bishop is seated before an altar. He lays his hands upon your head and gives you the spirit of the community or, as the French call it, the community's "esprit de corps," which you come to discover is none other than that same Holy Spirit sent by God the Father into the church after the Lord's resurrection. Having received this Holy Spirit, you exchange the peace of Christ with your new fellow Christians and together with them offer bread and wine upon the altar. Then, for the first time in your life, you witness and take part in the performance of those secret rites known as the Christian Mysteries, for which Christians are persecuted daily and in defense of which many of your closest friends have died. Yet these rites turn out to be so very simple. The bishop blesses bread and wine, saying over them the words by which Jesus proclaimed that they were His body and blood, and then you are fed with "The body of Christ, the bread of heaven" and you drink "The blood of Christ, the cup of salvation."

That is all there is to it, but by the time it is finished a new day has dawned and a new life begun. You know in your heart of hearts that what has been celebrated today is not just the day of Christ's resurrection but your own resurrection as well. In the waters of baptism you have been buried with Him, and from these waters you have risen to new life. To live that new life a new Spirit has been poured into you, God the Holy Spirit who gives life to all the people of God. You have been joined to a new super-race and made a member of the very kingdom of heaven itself. In that kingdom you are sustained by other worldly food and drink that is none other than the resurrected body and blood of your God.

A New Spirit

This day of resurrection is only a beginning. In the days and years to come you will continue on your journey of faith, but sustained now by the Spirit of a new family and of a new nation. As St. Peter once told those who had just been baptized, "You are a royal nation, a holy priesthood, an amazing people" (1 Peter 2:9).

Somewhat like the way we are united to one another by a school spirit or team spirit, these early Christians were united by a special spirit governing the life of this new community into which they had been baptized, and their experience of its common life forced them to believe that this spirit was none other than God Himself, the Holy Spirit. In baptism, the old spirit of the world—which previously governed everything they did—had now been killed forever and the Holy Spirit had begun to take over their lives. For them the quality of their new life in the Spirit was the final evidence for faith and the only certain proof that the God discovered by the ancient Jews really is the one true God.

Those who were initiated into the church after Jesus' resurrection were forced to conclude that the Holy Spirit who animated this new body of Christ was the same God who had been working in Jesus from the beginning. And just as Jesus had played a part in the life of our humanity from the moment of His conception, so this same Holy Spirit—ruling the lives of His followers from the moment of their baptism—gave them a part to play in the divine life of God Himself. By offering their bread and wine, the result of all their labors, on the altar of Christian sacrifice, they themselves actually became the body and blood of their God through the transforming power of this same Holy Spirit. What Adam and Eve had been unable to do by themselves, these early Christians discovered had been done for them. Through their life in the church they had become as gods and that human desire to be divine—instead of ending in sin and death—now led to new life in the power of the resurrected Christ.

Through the Holy Spirit they had a new energy and a new strength. He led them into all truth so that now they saw everything from the new perspective of hope. They were able to do the works of sacrificial love that Jesus Himself had done and, as He had promised, they were able to do even greater works than these. As members of Jesus' resurrected body on earth they were no longer limited, as Jesus had been, by the confines of an individual neighborhood in a particular country at a single moment of time. By the power of the Holy Spirit, the new Christian community swiftly spread throughout the whole world, accomplishing in all places throughout the ages the wonderful works of God.

20

Where Do You Go from Here?

Those early Christians found themselves gradually transformed by a power they could not explain. They knew that the change within them could not have come through their own efforts, for that way had always led to disaster. Nor was it through the charisma of their church's leaders who, on the whole, were anything but charismatic, and it certainly was not created by some organized psychological gimmick because they did not have any in those days. It seemed obvious to them that this personal transformation could have come only about through the Holy Spirit they had received at their baptism when they were adopted into a new order of peace and love, a supernatural order created by the same Spirit on the Day of Pentecost when Mary and the apostles were gathered together in the upper room.

The personal experience of the transforming power of the Holy Spirit convinced these early Christians that Jesus was alive and well and working among them. But is it possible for us to have this same experience today? That Spirit which was given to the Christian church 2,000 years ago is by now so intermingled with the spirit of our everyday secular world that there seems no easy way to distinguish one from the other. No longer able to be plunged into a new way of life through some dramatic rite of initiation, it never occurs to most people that baptism makes them members of some special kind of Spirit-filled community, any more than going to the theater makes them members of a theater community. At best they may decide to become friends or even patrons of one or the other. In a church where ordination rather than baptism has become the new initiation rite and only the clergy are said to "enter the church," real membership is left to the professionals, and much of the talk about "lay ministry" does little more than merely treat the actively committed members of the church as though they were ordained clergy without pay.

It is possible, of course, to restore all the old initiation ceremonies. In many churches adults and children are baptized, confirmed, and receive their first holy communion at Easter Vigil services in the middle of the night, and this can be a very moving occasion in which the candidate gains a wonderful sense of receiving a Spirit not of this world, and of being lifted into the very presence of God. Yet, when the service of initiation is over, life in the church carries on exactly as before. There are no new mysteries that the candidate has not already experienced and, except for receiving communion, nothing in his life seems to change.

Baptism in the Spirit

Because Christian initiation these days rarely gives people any lasting experience of the power of the Holy Spirit, many Christians have started talking about a separate "baptism of the Spirit," and some actually claim that only those who have received this baptism are real Christians and true members of the church. Usually, they themselves have had some kind of powerful conversion experience, which has suddenly redirected their whole lives towards God, convincing them that even though they may not yet be very good Christians, their lives are empowered by a Spirit not of this world. An inner experience of the living God gives them a certainty which cannot be shaken by any kind of rational argument or personal disaster. Knowing already the active power of God in their lives, they do not need to read a book like this, nor are they inclined to think that anyone else need read it either. God, they believe, will not be known by any kind of evidence that I or anyone else can offer, but only through a personal conversion similar to their own.

For those who believe they have been baptized in the Holy Spirit— and there are many thousands of them—this experience is sufficient reason for entrusting their whole life to Jesus. It is of no help, however, to those who have never had such an experience and are yet desperately looking for some kind of meaning in their lives and still seeking the fulfillment of all their dreams and desires.

Nor does it answer the doubts of those who once believed they had such an experience but, either through the weight of everyday responsibilities and disappointments, or through the arguments of friends, or perhaps disillusionment with their fellow Christians, have gradually lost their original certainty of faith and become indifferent towards God and their fellow Christians. It is no good claiming that these people have given way to the devil, as is sometimes said. More often than not they fervently wish their original confidence could be restored, but are unable to find any way in which this can possibly happen. With nostalgia they look back to former happier times when for a moment it seemed as though God really was in his heaven and all was right with the world.

Perhaps you are one of these people. If so, the heart of Jesus goes out to you just as fervently as it does to the fully committed. Perhaps even more so. If Jesus is God the Creator, then surely He loves all the people He has made, and gives Himself to everyone with no conditions laid down and no strings attached. His Holy Spirit is available to everyone, so that we can all have that certainty of faith which, when reason operates solely on its own, forever remains an insubstantial hope.

That First Step

If you think it is possible that the Christian faith may be true, but still cannot find any way of being certain that it is, do not be afraid to take the first step on the pilgrimage of faith, and to test the spirits of the committed, whether or not they are of God. Become involved in the life of the Christian community; find out if over and above the spirit of dissension, bitterness, and pettiness that you find, there is also a spirit greater than these, a Holy Spirit which, at the end of the day, overcomes all opposition and all discouragement. Begin to talk to God as a real person, and instead of depending upon the uninformed hearsay of others, take advantage of every opportunity to learn firsthand what the Christian faith is really all about.

Then, when you have taken this first step, do not become discouraged if nothing changes in your life all at once. For some people God's action apparently hits them like a bolt of lightning, but for most of us there is only a gradual process of recognition. Persevere in your search for faith, but always with the hope that the time will come when you can commit yourself totally to the God of the ancient Jews, fully revealed in the living Christ by the Holy Spirit working within you.

A Faith for Skeptics
Order Form

Postal orders: 204 N. Rosemont Ave.*
Dallas, Texas 75208

Telephone orders: (214) 941-3872*

E-mail orders: fjheidt8914@sbcglobal.net*
*Please send a check of money order when ordering from the above locations.

Please send *A Faith for Skeptics* to:

Name: _____

Address: _____

City: _____ State: _____

Zip: _____

Telephone: (_____) _____

Book Price: $11.95

Shipping: $3.00 for the first book and $1.00 for each additional book to
cover shipping and handling within US, Canada, and Mexico.
International orders add $6.00 for the first book and $2.00 for
each additional book.

Or order from:
ACW Press
85334 Lorane Hwy
Eugene, OR 97405

(800) 931-BOOK

or contact your local bookstore